Mental Training for Skydiving and Life

A Mind/Body/Spirit Training Program for Achieving Peak Performance in Skydiving and Life

John J. DeRosalia,
CSW, C.Ht.

SkyMind Publishers
West Hurley, New York

ISBN: 0-9707763-0-6

Editor: Char Wait

Artist and Cover Designer: Monica Weiss

Cover photo of skydivers exiting airplane by Brent Finley:
www.brentfinley.com

John J. DeRosalia * PO Box 283 * West Hurley, NY 12491
USA
Phone and Fax: (845) 331-8384
Email: skymind@pobox.com

To my father, Salvatore DeRosalia, for teaching me
love and courage the hard way.
To my mother, Dorothy.
To my children, John and Sal.
To my brothers, Frank, Tom and Joe.
To my best friends, Jim, John and Reine.
To Mandy and Demi.

To Stephanie
For your quiet beauty, love and endless compassion.

To the loved ones who've carried me for so much of
my life.

To my higher power for the gift of all these
wonderful people.

CONTENTS

Acknowledgments

There are so many I owe so much to. In order of their appearance in assisting me with this project: Thank you Penny and Landmark Education for getting me started. To my dear friend Ellen Reed, for your undying belief in me and for agreeing to be my first test dummy. I'm so glad you survived. (At least I think you did.) To Craig Girard and Kirk Verner for your guidance and example and for steering me in the right direction. To Jack Jefferies for your leadership and inspiration and for opening up a vast world of possibilities in skydiving. To Joey Jones, Dawn English, Doug Parks, Chris Erwin, Neal Houston and Dave Timko (all one-time members of FX), for having the courage and foresight to work with me, for giving me your trust, and for teaching me so much about the competitive aspects of this sport. To all my friends at Skydive University—Rob Laidlaw, Craig Buxton, Anne Maxwell, and Debbie Bull—for your commitment to teaching, sharing and learning, for your open-mindedness and leadership, and for giving me the privilege of being part of The Search. To Joe Trinko for your friendship and support and for reminding me over and over again how valuable my work is. To Peter Allum: your being inspires me to never stop growing and reaching and loving every minute of it. Thank you Monica, for appearing at the eleventh hour to design a great cover. To Ana, Janet, and Soraya for giving so much of your lives and time.

To Char Wait, my very generous friend and editor, this couldn't have been done without you. The time, patience and love you've given to this project will always be cherished by me.

A special thanks to all of the skydivers and teams I've had the opportunity to coach over the past few years and to my friends and teachers at the Blue Sky Ranch in New York. I hope you've learned as much from me as I have from you.

Tina—it was a great first year, wasn't it?

And to the many people whose names don't appear on this page, who've given me so much—I sincerely thank you.

Preface

Anyone compelled into the competitive arena will encounter the greatest challenge a human being can face: the current of our own thought. Although we possess an awesome power to create our reality, few ever learn the simple mental techniques that accomplish outrageous results.
If we can perfectly envision our mastery,
then mastery becomes our domain.
Ellen Reed

Shortly after I began skydiving in 1997 I had two sudden realizations. The first was that skydiving is predominantly a mental activity in spite of the high degree of physical skill and dexterity that's required as one progresses in the sport. I like the way baseball great Yogi Berra put it: "Ninety percent of hitting is mental. The other fifty percent is physical."

Secondly, I noticed the absence of mental training in our sport. Visit any Olympic village and you'll find countless sport psychologists and mental training coaches in attendance. In fact all of the major sports—baseball, football, basketball, tennis, golf, etc.—utilize various mental training programs as an integral part of their training curriculum. In skydiving this is conspicuously absent. The literature barely touches on the subject and, even when it does, it makes little mention of the exciting groundbreaking technology in peak performance that has been developing over the past twenty-five years.

As a psychotherapist and mental training coach by profession, this afforded me a unique opportunity. I had already fallen in love with skydiving and the thought of being able to integrate it into my professional life was thrilling. I immediately began to systematically study and research the current literature on performance enhancement training both in and out of sports, and I began interviewing some of the best skydivers in the world. My goal was to develop a handful of practical and effective mental training techniques designed specifically for skydiving. I decided that since my research was experimental at best, and I had no idea how receptive the skydiving community would be, I would begin by offering this information in seminar fashion to a few small drop zones in remote parts of the country. A small audience would be a good way to start.

After six months of intensive work I was ready. I had learned a lot through developing and adapting a number of techniques—some of which were original and some of which had already been time-proven in other sports and arenas—and I had also begun experimenting on willing skydivers with excellent results. I then wrote to a few small drop zones around the country offering to conduct free seminars, but no one responded. I decided to follow up with personal phone calls, but again no one seemed interested. One evening, while sharing my plight with Craig Girard and Kirk Verner at an Airspeed skills camp in New York, they suggested I contact Tim Wagner, the DZ manager at Skydive Arizona. When I called Tim he immediately invited me to give my seminar the following month at the 1998 US Nationals. So much for a small audience at an insignificant drop zone.

The seminar was a complete success. In fact, I was asked to give a second one the next day—again a success. I learned that many skydivers are eager to train mentally but simply don't know how or what to do or where to go for information. A few of the top teams and individual competitors that I met there were using various mental training tools, and one team in particular had a fairly solid program in place, but no one had integrated the best and most current research on mental training into a comprehensive system specifically designed for skydiving.   So I accepted the challenge and began the most ambitious project of my life.

A little over two years later this book is the result—and an incredible two years it's been. I have learned far more than I ever expected, and many times, just when I thought I was done writing, I learned something else that demanded inclusion. So now that it's finally complete (or is it?) I see that it's just the beginning.

This book really just scratches the surface—there is so much more to learn. The formidable task of creating and applying mental training techniques in this extraordinary sport of ours will continue for many years to come. I welcome any suggestions, comments, and criticisms you care to share with me.

There is a vitality, a life force, an energy,
a quickening that is translated through you into
action,
and because there is only one of you in all of time, this
expression is
unique.
And if you block it, it will never exist through any
other medium and   it will be lost.
The world will not have it.

It is not your business to determine how good it is
nor how valuable
nor how it compares with other expressions.
It is your business to keep it yours clearly and
directly,
          to keep the channel open.

Martha Graham, quoted by Agnes Demille,
Martha: the Life and Work of Martha Graham

Introduction

If it's possible, it's been done.
If it's impossible, it will be done.
Steve Wallenda

In 1954 an event occurred that shocked the world and expanded the boundaries of human consciousness forever. Roger Bannister of England, an athlete who refused to abandon an impossible dream, ran the mile in three minutes and fifty-nine seconds in a race that will never be forgotten by those who saw it. Until that day it was believed that no human being was capable of running a mile in less than four minutes. It was an accepted and well-known medical fact that man was not biologically or structurally designed to run at such speeds—a fact that Roger Bannister chose to ignore.

His belief, conviction, and *knowing,* allowed his vision to extend beyond the confines of "reality." And while his physical achievement was truly amazing, it paled in comparison to the psychological impact this achievement would have on the world. Within days, the four-minute barrier was broken again by another runner. And two weeks later it was broken again. And then again, and again, and again...

Why, suddenly, were so many athletes performing a feat that only weeks before had been impossible? The answer, of course, is that they no longer believed it was impossible. Their old reality had been shattered and their present reality had taken on new parameters, all because someone had a dream and refused to believe an illusion.

What are your boundaries? What secret convictions do you hold that stop you from realizing your dream? Do you think you're not smart enough, or skilled enough? Do you need proof that it can be done? Is what you want only achievable by those "special others" because they have qualities and abilities far beyond yours?

Mental training for peak performance is a process that leads to an interesting phenomenon called *change*. Change is something that either occurs or it doesn't. It's one of the few things in this world that's black and white. There's no gray area. If it occurs a little, it's change. If it occurs a lot, it's change. But there's no in-between.

Change can be either large or small. What matters is not the amount, but the direction. Generally speaking, small change now is better than big change later, because later has a way of never showing up.

There's also no such thing as "trying" to change. If you're trying to change, you're not changing—you're "trying" to change. You can jump out of a plane or you can not jump out of a plane. You can exercise every day or you can not exercise every day. But you cannot "try" to jump out of a plane or "try" to exercise every day. You either do it or you don't. The paradox of change is that the harder you try, the less you change; the less you change, the harder you try. And so this book is not about trying to change. It's about changing.

There's a story of a woman bringing her son to Gandhi because she was concerned that the boy was eating too much sugar. She asked Gandhi if he would instruct her son to stop eating sugar.

Gandhi looked at the boy and then at the mother and told them to go home and come back in a week. When they returned, he took the boy aside and spoke to him for a moment. He then brought him back to the mother saying: "I've told him not to eat any more sugar." With a puzzled expression on her face the woman looked at Gandhi and said: "I don't understand—why didn't you tell him that last week when we were here?" Gandhi looked at her and said, "I needed to stop eating sugar first."

I can only teach what I've first learned myself; I can only take you as far as my own experience has gone. To attempt to do anything else is to "talk the talk" but not "walk the walk." I don't trust people whose actions don't match their words, and I don't expect that you do either. I want you to know that I've personally experienced all of the training methods and techniques covered in this book. For me they've opened countless doors and created opportunities that I never knew existed. They've also deepened my insight and enhanced my effectiveness as a coach.

I ask that you read this book with a beginner's mind in a playful spirit of discovery and experimentation. The real masters I've encountered in my life are humble, joyful, and driven by a childlike curiosity. They continually embrace every opportunity to learn.

I ask that you "check your guns at the door" so to speak, that you suspend judgment on any method, technique, or concept here until you've tried it. If something doesn't work for you, please feel free to toss it or tuck it away for a later date. In other words, take what you want and leave the rest. Just have a good time doing it.

This book is for skydivers and non-skydivers alike. Used correctly, it can make a difference in your life as well as your sport, and in fact any notion of separation between the two is illusory anyway. My wish for you is that as you work the methods and techniques contained here, you will marvel at the inseparable nature of life and sport and learn to deeply appreciate their interdependence. You will find that as you work one you work the other, and discover that every waking experience can be transformed into a performance enhancement training opportunity, if you allow it. The choice however, is up to you.

CHAPTER 1

A Paradigm for Change

Life is a series of wonderful opportunities,
brilliantly disguised as impossible situations.

While there are clearly exceptions to every rule, a true champion is someone who demonstrates outstanding ability both in and out of his or her area of expertise and views every situation as an opportunity for growth and transformation. To be remarkable in your specialty alone is simply to be a skilled practitioner. A champion, however, perceives life itself as the court on which the real game is played and the fundamental skills learned.

Without a doubt, life offers countless varieties of experiences in all sizes, shapes, and colors. Some we love, while others push us to our edge and beyond. If growth is our ultimate goal, then all experiences have the power to teach. Anything becomes possible when we are willing to journey to an unknown destination and risk experiencing something new, not knowing if it will thrill us or kill us or maybe both.

When it comes to external experiences (activities), this kind of "living on the edge" is acceptable and even preferable for many people, especially those of us engaged in high-risk sports. However, when it comes to internal experiences (feelings and emotions), the large majority of us would rather do something else, anything else, than explore that terrain. All too often the footing on that path seems just a bit too treacherous.

Since childhood I've had a fear of heights and flying. In spite of this (actually because of this) I began skydiving a few years ago to distract myself from a deeply painful situation in my life. I figured that jumping out of an airplane would at least temporarily take my mind off of my emotional distress, and if my parachute didn't open, well, that was okay too. I wasn't particularly thrilled with the way life was treating me anyway. As I reflect on it now, I realize that it was easier for me to jump out of a plane two miles high than it was for me to sit on the ground with my feelings. Given those two options at that point, the decision was clear.

It takes effort to experience raw, uncomfortable emotions as they occur in the moment—to look at them, feel them, touch them, taste them, and just sit with them quietly. It takes courage to sustain and integrate those emotions—to hold them close and examine the effect they're having on our body and behavior without shrinking back or pushing them away. Our natural aversion to discomfort prompts us to take some kind of action in order to minimize its impact. But generally speaking, the greater our resistance, the worse our discomfort becomes.

We resort to our most "brilliant thinking." We try to rationalize or intellectualize our fears and uncomfortable emotions away. We get lost in doing and fixing and changing things out of our desire to make life work the way we think it should. The thought of stopping to listen for a moment—just listen without acting—rarely crosses our minds. Yet this very simple practice of awareness can gently lead us out of the maze of emotional confusion. At times it's our only hope of finding a solution. Joseph Jaworski talks about this in terms of commitment when he writes of the "integrity of surrender." In his book, *Synchronicity: The Inner Path of Leadership,* he says: "I actualize my commitment by listening, out of which my 'doing' arises. Sometimes the greatest acts of commitment involve doing nothing but sitting and waiting until I just know what to do next" (12).

Internal listening and the expression of a wide range of emotions is discouraged in certain sports, especially those in which posturing and bravado are subtle requirements for participation. These sports have a tendency to judge certain feelings and emotions as signs of weakness. (This is an observation, not a criticism.) In this context, the notion of mental training is sometimes misunderstood and viewed as a violation or contradiction of our purpose in the sport, or at best an unnecessary sensitivity exercise that we could all do without.

While some sports place high value on developing mental abilities through self-awareness, others clearly don't, especially when emotional sensitivity is the very thing we may be trying to avoid through our participation. Ultimately, our reluctance to explore this emotional arena restricts our growth in the sport we love and desire improvement in.

The converse is also true. With regard to skydiving, I've never met a community of people more capable of living in the moment and expressing passion for life. Skydivers are an amazing group of people, willing to risk everything for the sake of an experience. But clearly there are dimensions within sports that require different kinds of risks.

Exploration of the "internal experience" is an absolute requirement for peak performance and will lead us to a finer, more acute edge with exciting new possibilities. As we learn to be comfortable in what was once uncharted territory, we'll begin to achieve what was formerly inconceivable.

The French poet and philosopher Guillaume Apollinaire
expresses it well:

> Come to the edge.
> We can't, we're afraid.
> Come to the edge.
> We can't, we'll fall.
> Come to the edge.
>
> And they came.
> And he pushed them.
>
> And they flew.

Step One: Awareness

All learning rests on awareness in one form or another. Mental
training in particular utilizes conscious self-awareness as its
foundation for creating possibility from experience. The better
we understand our mental and emotional machinery, the more
effectively we can respond to any situation with spontaneity and
flexibility.   Ignorance may be bliss, but it's certainly not
productive or efficient. At best, it fosters denial and prevents us
from realizing our true potential by blocking access to the tools
we need to actualize our goals.

You wouldn't dream of jumping a rig you hadn't
checked out thoroughly (I hope). You wouldn't consider flying
a canopy without knowing something about its condition and
performance characteristics (again, I hope). As skydivers, we
place high value on having the best equipment and are generally
willing to spend top dollar to get it. But unfortunately, we tend
to overlook our mental equipment. We accept it as is, without
really knowing exactly how it functions or how efficiently it's
operating at any given point in time.

Most of us underestimate the degree to which our feelings, emotions, attitudes, thoughts, moods, and beliefs affect and actually guide our performance. We forget (or simply refuse to believe) that mental conditioning is a major factor in determining any outcome. Raw skill alone, without mental training or toughness, is like a finely tuned race car running on low-grade gasoline; when it malfunctions and fails to rise to the occasion, we're left bewildered and wondering what went wrong. We then compound the problem even further by looking in the wrong place for the answers.

In his book, *The New Toughness Training For Sports,* James E. Loehr explains:

> The reason emotion is so important is its connection to arousal. Emotions are biochemical events in the brain that can lead to a cascade of powerful changes in the body. . . . The body is physical; talent and skill are physical; emotions are neurochemical events and are therefore physical; and thinking and visualizing are electrochemical events in the brain and are also physical. Athletes make the mistake of believing that what they think, particularly negative thinking, has little effect on their performance. . . Well, lets get this straight once and for all: thoughts and feelings are physical stuff too; they are just as real and every bit as fundamental to achievement as talent and skill. (7-8)

Loehr's point is powerful and well made. All too often we see highly skilled individual athletes as well as top notch teams turn in a substandard performance, knowing full well that their breakdown had nothing to do with technical skill or ability and everything to do with attitude and mind set. But they couldn't see at the time what others around them could see so clearly. They were blinded by their own denial.

This scenario is commonplace in most of our lives. We have all failed to achieve a goal at one time or another due to a lack of mental training or toughness. The question is, were we honest enough to acknowledge our shortcoming(s) and make the necessary changes for our next goal, or did we refuse to see our part in the problem and instead make excuses by blaming someone or something for our inadequacy? If we did the latter then we probably wound up looking for solutions in the wrong places.

When we get caught in this trap we're generally left confused and hoping that our problem, whatever it is, will eventually clear itself up on its own. We become like the person in the dark looking under a streetlight for his lost car keys. When a passerby asks where he lost them he says "down the block." When they ask why he's not looking down the block for them, he says, "because there's more light here." It's been said that *it's not our problems that get us into trouble—it's our solutions.* It is our tendency to gravitate towards places that are comfortable and familiar that causes us to overlook the places where the real answers might be found. That's why "the road less traveled" is less traveled.

Self-awareness training is a vital tool for achieving peak performance. Without it we are left searching endlessly for answers where they don't exist. Similarly, if we are fully aware of the value but have no understanding of how to access the tools of self-awareness, we are equally disadvantaged. In either case the outcome is greatly reduced potential.

What is Awareness?

To be aware is to be mindful. It involves listening to the activity of your mind and body to discover what you're experiencing both mentally and physically. If awareness could speak it would ask:

> What's going on *NOW?*   What feelings, emotions, thoughts and sensations am I experiencing right now? What am I really telling myself about this situation?

Am I confident, energized, relaxed and focused or am I
annoyed, anxious, fatigued, tense, and overly sensitive,
etc.? Can I feel how my body is responding physically?
What muscles are contracting? Can I feel their
tightness? Is my stomach a little uneasy? Are my
palms sweaty? Am I in touch with any physical
sensations or have I dissociated from my body at this
moment? (Many of us fall into this last category, never
having paid much attention to the subtle physical
reactions that accompany emotional events.)

Every emotion has a physical counterpart, and every change in
physiology alters our emotions. Tension manifests itself in the
body; stress and tension always express themselves in physical
symptoms. The body continually responds to each and every
life experience on both a mental and physical level. In addition,
each level may contain both positive and negative responses.
For instance, tension for one person at a given time might
mobilize their competitive juices and increase their reaction
time and response capabilities. For that same person at another
point in time this tension might decrease their overall flexibility
by contracting certain muscles. This could easily restrict
mobility, resulting in reduced speed, inefficient movement, or
erratic fall rate. The consequent damage to performance could
be major, as in funneling an exit, or minor (and possibly even
go unnoticed) as in a slightly decreased reaction time. But even
the smallest impairment can make the difference between
winning and losing—between first place and no place at all.

Awareness Exercise

Goal:
To increase physical and psychological awareness and assess overall functioning ability, locate areas of mental, emotional and physical stress, and provide an indication of arousal levels. (Level of arousal refers to the combined state of physical and emotional excitement at any given moment. The ideal level of arousal is that place where these combined energies afford optimum performance—that delicate, balanced point between high and low psychic energy.)

It is best to do this exercise in writing. It can be used anytime, anywhere and can be especially useful just prior to an important event.

Time Element:
This can be done in 5 minutes if necessary.

Procedure:
Find a quiet place where you won't be disturbed and begin by taking a mental/emotional inventory. Simply write down all of the thoughts and feelings that you're having about this situation. Pay attention to your internal conversation—what you're saying to yourself about what's going on. Just list whatever comes to mind even if some of it sounds ridiculous. You're the only one who's going to see it, so be honest.

Next, begin scanning your body and take a physical inventory. Starting at your toes, systematically work your way up your body through your feet, shins, calves, thighs, buttocks, hips, abdomen, lower back, upper back, chest, neck, face, head, shoulders, arms and hands. Notice any sensations, pleasant or unpleasant, that you become aware of. Pay particular attention to areas of tenseness, stiffness, soreness and any internal activity going on in your stomach, chest, head, etc. Be aware of your breathing. This is extremely important; your breathing can be a real barometer of your overall condition.   Are you breathing from your chest or stomach, through your nose or mouth? Are your breaths deep or shallow, regular or erratic? Just notice all of these things without changing any of them at this point.

Next, separate your mental and physical reactions into positives (functional) and negatives (dysfunctional). You now have a complete physical and psychological inventory and can see what areas need to be addressed. Very often the mere action of doing this exercise reduces or eliminates negative feelings and sensations and relaxes muscles.

The following is an example of an Awareness Exercise done by a skydiver just prior to an AFF evaluation.

MENTAL AWARENESS

Positive
Feel prepared
Determined to do well
Able to visualize and
   focus on routine

Negative
Arousal level a bit too high
Worried about being criticized
   and embarrassed
Remembering past mistakes
   and failures
Annoyed at myself for having
   performance anxiety

PHYSICAL AWARENESS

Positive
Feel strong and energized
Breathing a little shallow
   but otherwise normal

Negative
Tightness in neck and lower
   back
Upset stomach
Sweaty palms
Underarm perspiration

Step Two: Acceptance

The notion of acceptance is frequently overlooked or completely bypassed by most of us in the hope of producing change quickly. Once we acknowledge an area in our lives that needs improvement, the inclination is to immediately take action to eliminate the problem. While this may sound like a great idea, internal change usually requires an additional step, especially when we're attempting to change a deeply ingrained pattern of behavior or a personality trait.

This step is acceptance of myself as I am—right now—in the present moment. Not the way I'd like to be, or hope to be, or wish to be, but just the way I am. Once I can reach the point where I'm able to say, "Like it or not, this is me," then change becomes possible.

The fascinating thing about internal change is that I can never *make* it happen. I can, however, *allow* it to happen by creating the proper atmosphere. A flower may grow if I prepare the soil, plant the seed, fertilize and water it, and expose it to the sun. But I cannot make it grow.   Similarly, I can make all of the conditions right for internal change to occur in my life, but I cannot make it occur. I can, however, allow it to.

In his book, *Playing in the Zone: Exploring the Spiritual Dimensions of Sports,* Andrew Cooper describes the phenomenon of the "zone" or "flow" in much the same way. He refers to the zone—an elevated, almost supernormal state of being where amazing feats are accomplished almost effortlessly—using Csikszentmihalyi's defining characteristics of "deep concentration, highly efficient performance, emotional buoyancy, a heightened sense of mastery, a lack of self-consciousness, and self-transcendence" (21).   They both agree that an athlete, no matter how great, cannot enter the zone at will. It is a state that seems to occur on its own when a number of preconditions are met and the athlete is not consciously attempting to reach it.   In fact, once an athlete becomes consciously aware of being in the zone, it mysteriously disappears. How interesting that the highest plateau a human being can attain is only possible in the absence of any attempt to reach it.

Many of us, particularly those involved in competing or performing on some level, become overly self-critical when we encounter personal faults or shortcomings. We use this criticism as a weapon to motivate ourselves to improve and not repeat the same mistakes. But in most cases, self-criticism actually reinforces the problem we are trying to eliminate. Occasionally we are able to effect change in this way but at a very high price—we forfeit our enjoyment of the activity we're engaged in. We trade our love of what we're doing for the promise of a better performance. We sacrifice the joy of the journey for what appears to be a higher goal—winning.

The problem with using harsh, negative motivation on ourselves is that it undermines the very reason for our involvement in the sport to begin with. It takes the socially prestigious goal of winning and places it above all else, including joy and happiness. We wouldn't be skydiving to begin with if it weren't for the pleasure and fun we derive from participation. And so we need to ask ourselves two questions.

Is winning worth all this?

Is it worth being morbidly serious all the time in hopes that we'll be rewarded with improvement and higher scores? Is it worth having to punish ourselves every time we don't meet our own expectations? Self-criticism by definition is anger directed inward. It's a brutal and misguided attempt to manipulate and control ourselves though the use of force and the threat of punishment. When criticism speaks, the message we hear internally is:

> I have no respect for you the way you are. Your mistakes/imperfections have greatly diminished your value as a person. You'd better change and change

immediately if you want me to treat you well. And until
you do I'll continue to criticize and torment you.

I've heard it said, "If anyone ever treated me the way I treat myself, I'd beat him senseless." The truth for most of us is that if somebody other than ourselves were to make those kinds of demands on us, we would promptly end the relationship.

If you think this kind of internal conversation is an exaggeration, I can assure you it's not. I've heard it in my own head countless times, and I've personally worked with hundreds of very talented, capable, and extremely successful people over the years who have been tortured and driven by the same voice. And none of us were crazy—or maybe we all were. Actually, we were just well trained as children and carried certain dysfunctional learning patterns into adulthood. We were raised in a system, either at home or school or both, that fostered a rigid style of teaching based on the belief that children are fundamentally lazy and unmotivated and if left to their own devices will never do anything worthwhile that requires effort. We were taught that motivation needs to come "from behind" with a very unpleasant stimulus, the most painful of all being the threat of rejection, condemnation, and abandonment. And so as adults, many of us continue to inflict this emotional pain on ourselves as a form of motivation. And yes, pain and rejection are motivators. They can certainly make me sing and dance. But over time their effects are devastating. Not only do they kill whatever fun we're having, but they're second rate motivators at best.

Acceptance is a powerful and dynamic force.
It motivates by keeping the fun alive. Consequently, we improve at a more rapid pace because we're not wasting our time and energy doing battle with ourselves. The problem is this: whenever anybody (especially myself) threatens me in any way, the one thing that is absolutely certain is that I'll resist (or I'll get even). Although I may eventually give in, it won't

happen without a fight. Initially, it may look like I've surrendered, but in fact I've gone underground. I'm preparing my forces for the impending engagement, and all hell is about to break loose. I'm telling myself, "Nobody treats me like that and gets away with it." I resort to my most effective weapon— sabotage.

While this may sound ridiculous, please believe me that it's a familiar struggle that occurs internally in many athletes— even world-class athletes—and there's a good chance it goes on in you to some extent. In fact, it's one of the major causes of burnout.

The truth is that negative motivation sometimes works temporarily, but it ultimately malfunctions over time. Paradoxically, instead of our effort and energy leading to great improvements, our performance instead begins to deteriorate. We spin our wheels and get nowhere. We then respond to this disappointment by applying even more pressure to ourselves, and as the pressure increases so does our stress and resistance. And so it goes.

Occasionally, in spite of all this wasted effort, we sometimes do succeed—only to win the booby prize. We arrive at our destination exhausted and find that our victory is totally meaningless and devoid of any pleasure. We're holding the cherished prize but feel miserable and worn out. We paid a fortune for this experience both literally and figuratively and now find it worthless.

On the other hand, acceptance provides a gentle, productive path that's amazingly effective at facilitating change. It also allows us to grow and take risks in a nonjudgmental atmosphere, free of fear and self-criticism.

To cultivate acceptance we begin by making a decision to not judge ourselves.
Instead we treat ourselves kindly regardless of our shortcomings and limitations. This doesn't mean that we don't care about winning or improving. Quite the contrary, we act this way

because we care a great deal. In fact, we continue to vigorously assess our performance skills and be firm and unyielding in our commitment to grow and change.   But we do so with compassion, because we know that self-criticism only fosters resistance and solidifies unwanted behavior. We know that if we judge ourselves for our imperfections, our mind won't be as willing in the future to bring new imperfections to our attention for fear of being judged again. And so the message contained in self-acceptance is clear—we can be trusted with the fruits of our own awareness.

Step Three: Action

Training is creating a plan of action and following through on that plan with discipline and courage. It requires setting a goal, developing the means to achieve it, and making a firm commitment to pursue that goal until we reach it or decide to revise it. Results usually come to those who persevere and enjoy the process.

Discipline
Webster's New Universal Dictionary defines discipline as:
1) training that develops self-control, character, or orderliness and efficiency, and 2) a system of rules and methods. . . .

The word "discipline" has gotten a bad reputation over the past few decades. Discipline is not about force, oppression, domination, or pain. In fact, when discipline is properly applied, our lives become easier rather than more difficult. Discipline is user-friendly and probably more than any other mental quality is essential for achieving peak performance.
      Discipline in mental training refers to an inner quality that keeps one focused, in motion, and goal oriented, and demands adherence to the training plan. The possibility that the

goal might never be achieved is irrelevant. Discipline is the act of carrying out a plan of action and putting forth a genuine effort regardless of the possible outcome.

Discipline is honoring your word and maintaining your commitment in spite of how you may feel at any given moment.

If you've agreed to a training regimen that involves waking at six a.m., meditating for twenty minutes, and then jogging for two miles, your commitment to discipline will keep you in that regimen. If your alarm goes off on Tuesday morning and you consider going back to sleep because you're not in the mood to get up, discipline will get you up in spite of your mood.

Discipline is action, not good intentions.

If your team is scheduled to meet at nine a.m., then discipline will get you there on time. Showing up at nine-thirty means there's been a break in discipline. That you had every intention of being there on time is nice, but it doesn't excuse your lateness. Most of us have been disappointed enough by well-intentioned people in our lives. We don't need to disappoint ourselves with the same good intentions.

Discipline is no excuses.

That doesn't mean perfection, but it does mean no excuses. It means owning your behavior, acknowledging your mistakes, recognizing lapses in self-control, admitting when you've fallen short on your promises to yourself and others, *and then doing something about it.*

Discipline means *thinking* before you commit to something.

Talk to friends, loved ones, and coaches—do extensive research if you have to—and get all the information you need about a subject ahead of time, because once you make a commitment to do something, you're bound by discipline to follow through. If you don't want to make a commitment, then don't. That's really okay. Certainly don't allow yourself to be pressured into making a commitment that you really don't want to make. There's nothing wrong with saying you're not ready, willing, or able to take on additional responsibility.

Discipline is realizing the importance of your responsibility and allegiance to yourself and to your word.
If you've agreed to do A, B, and C to get to point D, then discipline demands that you do just that. Besides, unless you're willing to follow through with a plan, how else will you know if you created one that works? If you do A, B, and C and never get to point D, then you at least have the distinction of knowing that you maintained discipline and did your best. And contrary to what some might say, doing your best really does count, although losing is never enjoyable.   But regardless of the outcome, knowing that you gave one hundred percent reflects integrity, however disappointing the loss may be.

What we usually call failure is simply unwanted results. Realize instead that what you got was feedback and not failure. You learned that A, B, and C did not get you to point D. If you decide to try again you've already acquired some very valuable information and a new starting point.

Discipline is your best friend and protector.
Healthy discipline is about encouragement rather than punishment. It is an inner voice that continually reminds you of your goals and the steps required to reach them. Sometimes this voice needs to be loud and demanding in order to get your attention and remind you of the consequences of not following through on your training plan. Like any good friend or coach it knows the heavy price of regret and remorse that comes from lack of success due to laziness, procrastination, or poor self-control.

Courage

Courage is the willingness to act in the presence of fear or discomfort. It is not the absence of fear that signifies courage but rather the response to it. Learning to swim is not a courageous act for someone who loves the water, but it is for someone who fears it. It always takes courage to face a fear head on.

If we're willing to be honest, fear for most of us is a constant traveling companion. What varies most from one person to another is not the amount or degree of fear that we experience but rather the particular things we're afraid of. I know lots of people who routinely risk their lives in one way or another but are terrified in situations that involve the possibility of emotional rejection or embarrassment. There are those who can jump out of a plane two miles above the earth, but cringe in terror at the thought of public speaking, the number one fear in this country. How many of us are afraid of failure? Fear of failure is the single greatest cause of stress, burnout, and performance anxiety there is. How many of us are even more afraid of success? That particular fear is so disguised that we usually cover it up by convincing ourselves that it's really failure we're afraid of. We ask ourselves, "Who in their right mind would be afraid of success?" You'd be surprised.

Courage is a quality that must be developed and maintained; it is a skill that requires practice and repetition to master.

Courage is not an inherent quality that we are either born with or not. It is an attribute that needs to be nurtured and developed over time. Courage doesn't develop easily and requires practice, patience, and a great deal of trial and error learning.

If we want to demonstrate courage in sport, then we need to practice it daily in our lives. One way to do this is by welcoming every obstacle and hardship as an opportunity for growth. Another is by developing a positive relationship to failure. Courage demands the perseverance to "fail" over and over again and still keep trying in the belief that failure is the step that immediately precedes success.

Courage is the strength to share "who I am" with another in fellowship.
Truly, no one is an island. It takes great courage to be willing to see ourselves as we are and share that with another human being. To admit our faults or limitations to only ourselves is helpful but may not be complete. Very often, in order to transcend a problem, we need to share it with at least one other person.

Resistance to doing this can be another form of fear and self-rejection, and genuine lasting change can't occur without full self-acceptance. Besides, honest self-disclosure is a gift to those we share ourselves with as well as an opportunity to receive feedback. And, it gives others permission to be themselves. Hiding our imperfections out of shame or embarrassment will only drive these perceived flaws underground and make them harder to access in the future. They'll become secrets, and secrets always have a way showing up and causing problems later on. We may be able to fool other people temporarily, but we always know the truth.

Make no mistake—mental training is hard work. It involves inner change, and for most human beings that's a difficult and fearful process, although we'd rather not admit it. We think we really do want to change to improve our lives and to become the best skydivers possible; we think we are willing to do whatever it takes to make it happen. However, these thoughts are not necessarily true. A part of us may be willing, but other parts may have major reservations. We've been living and acting in a certain manner for years and may not believe we're capable of change. We know who we are and who we've come to be over time. Can we be anything else? Can we really trust this process? Discipline and courage are the tools that allow us to try.

CHAPTER 2

Mental Pictures and Images

We must be the change we wish to see.
Gandhi

If I ask you what you did last night, or yesterday, or what you're going to do next week; if I ask you what color your car is, or how you plan to spend your next vacation; if I tell you not to think of your left elbow; the only way you can process any of these thoughts is to first imagine or picture them in your mind. For instance, to tell me how many chairs you have in your living room, you first have to envision your room and then count the number of chairs in it. To tell me the color of your car you have to picture your car and see its color. In order to comprehend a future event like a vacation, you have to begin by selecting a vacation spot from a list of possible places you hold in your memory, and then create a picture of where you plan to go and what you plan to do there. Most of our thinking ultimately turns out to be a combination of remembering and creating. But in either case, our mind is producing pictures and images and flashing them on our mental screen, either slowly or at incredible speeds.

It's as if our brain has a huge video library where something is always playing. In our thought-life we go from one image to the next, to the next, to the next, forever. There is always a next thought on the heels of the one before it. If you don't believe me, stop reading this for sixty seconds and think of nothing. Go ahead, I'll wait.

So how did you do? It's impossible, right? In fact, in order for you to even understand the word nothing, you had to first think of what nothing is, and then try to make it happen. And so in order to think of nothing, you had to think of something called nothing. Your mind had to search for a picture or image to represent the concept we call nothing. It may sound complicated but it really isn't. It's just how we think. Because words and thoughts are abstract, we need to connect them to forms in order to make sense of them. The word beautiful, for instance, has no meaning unless you have something in mind to associate it with or compare it too. Consequently, we use pictures and images.

Our Minds Can't Process A Negative Command

"Don't think of a pink elephant sitting in the middle of a kitchen table." The only way to understand that request is to first picture a pink elephant sitting in the middle of a kitchen table. Then you have to forget that picture to follow the instruction. Which means you have to keep reminding yourself of what it is you need to forget. You have to keep the picture in mind and repeatedly tell yourself not to think about it. Sounds crazy, doesn't it? Not to mention that it's impossible. The connections happen so quickly we're not even aware they're occurring.

We do this with many things in our lives. We try to make ourselves forget painful or unpleasant memories by strong-arming" our minds and forcing ourselves not to think of something. But it just doesn't work that way. Mental force tactics have a tendency to backfire and strengthen the unwanted thought or image. But fortunately there is a method that works, even if only temporarily.

The Conscious Mind Can Only Hold One Thought At A Time

I can replace one thought with another any time I decide to. This is the same as saying that I can replace one mental picture with another. Instead of thinking of a pink elephant sitting in the middle of a table, I can do a math problem in my head, or see myself winning the million-dollar lottery, or remember a scene from my favorite movie, or imagine anything that I want as long as it's not the elephant. It's impossible for the conscious mind to hold two thoughts at the same time. I cannot think of a pink elephant and do a math problem in my head simultaneously. These thoughts may switch places very rapidly in my mind, giving the impression that they're both in there together, but they're not. One must go if I'm to think of the other.

Let's look at an example. You're coaching a little league baseball team and your star hitter has been consistently swinging too low and missing every pitch. The tendency would be to tell him "don't swing low" the next time he gets up at bat. However, the negative command, "don't swing low," will actually force him to picture himself swinging low. It will strengthen that image in his mind and increase his chances of swinging low next time. Knowing this, a wise coach will instruct him to "swing high," thereby replacing the unwanted picture with the desired picture. This also eliminates the effort, struggle, and wasted energy that the hitter would expend trying to force something out of his mind, which he can't do anyway. An informed coach knows that the player can't picture swinging low and high at the same time, so he redirects his thinking toward seeing the desired goal.

A recent skydiving situation comes to mind. A 4-way competitor brain-locked on the third point of his last skydive. Not wanting to make the same mistake on his next jump, he kept telling himself, "don't brain-lock again." In order for his mind to understand what he was saying, it had to keep replaying the error he wanted to avoid repeating. Without realizing it, he was actually strengthening the blueprint of his mistake every time he repeated this negative command to himself. He was unintentionally reinforcing the behavior he wanted to eliminate. With each further command it became stronger in his mind, and on the following jump he brain-locked again. In a sense, he had no choice. He had effectively programmed himself to do it.

We Create What We See

In my practice as a hypnotherapist I often encounter people who want to stop smoking, lose weight, or change something about themselves they're unhappy with.   Some think hypnosis can magically make them do things they really don't want to do, or change things they've been unable to change on their own. Regardless of what my clients are attempting to accomplish, I begin by asking if they can see themselves in the state of already having what they desire. If they want to quit smoking or lose weight I ask "Can you see yourself as a nonsmoker?" or "Can you see yourself as thin as you'd like to be?" I have them try to visualize themselves without their problem, as if they had already achieved their goal. If they can't actually see it in their mind, then they're not yet ready to make the change.

People often respond with, "I really want to be thin, but I can't see myself that way." This tells me they can only picture themselves in their present, overweight condition. If they can only see themselves as overweight and wanting to be thin, then they will constantly be creating a situation in their lives where they are always "in the process of getting thin." They just won't ever get there. Or worse, they'll get there but be so uncomfortable with the change that they'll sabotage their newfound success and go back to the way they used to be. They'll get stuck in a perpetual state of dieting and gaining weight and dieting again, over and over. While they may be unhappy being overweight, at least it is familiar, and familiar for most human beings is a comfortable place to be.

This is one of the biggest reasons why diets don't work. It's usually not the diet that's lacking. It's how we see ourselves that prevents us from changing. It's our inability and often our unwillingness to see ourselves as we want to be that keeps us repeating a dysfunctional, unproductive behavior.

Similarly, when athletes tell me they want to be world champions, my first question is "What does it feel like to be a world champion?" If they can't tell me, then they probably won't become one. They need to see it in their mind's eye so they can move toward it. They need to first create the mental blueprint and then follow it to arrive at their goal. Chances are if you think back to the times in your life when you have achieved something, you'll find that you saw yourself accomplishing it long before it actually happened.

Children are always doing this through fantasy and daydreams. They have no problem imagining great things for themselves when they grow up. They seem to know intuitively that "we create what we see," and have no reservations about creating big things.

Adults, however, have much difficulty in this area. Many of us stopped believing in our dreams long ago. Then we stopped dreaming altogether because we told ourselves, "They won't come true anyway, so why get excited about something that's not going to happen? Besides, I won't get hurt if I don't expect too much." Subsequently, many of us abandoned our fantasies and settled for routine and fairly uneventful lives. We thought, "Maybe dreams come true for other people but I'm just not lucky enough, or rich enough, or attractive enough, or educated enough, or talented enough, or young enough," etc. We created in ourselves the dis-ease of "we're not enough," and in doing so justified our mediocrity. We became entrenched in unhappy lives and satisfied with being powerless and insignificant because we just couldn't see ourselves succeeding. We said, "I'll believe it when I see it," when the real truth is exactly the opposite.

I'll See It When I Believe It

I recently had the privilege of attending a seminar given by Pete Allum from the 4-way team Sebastian XL. Pete is not only a world-class skydiver, but a gifted and dedicated coach as well. I watched in awe over a four day period as he coached a number of young skydivers during a Skydive University event called The Search. His boundless energy and enthusiasm were contagious as he infected his students with his love of skydiving.

At the seminar Pete talked about his early dreams of becoming a champion. He recalled how as a young teenager, years prior to making his first jump, he had covered the walls of his room with pictures and posters of all his skydiving heroes. "I would look around my room," he said with his arms wide open as if embracing his heroes, "and imagine myself as one of them. I was constantly dreaming of being a great skydiver. It was always on my mind." As he reminisced he radiated the glow and wonder of a teenage boy preparing to be a champion. As he shared his story his energy increased, his movements became more animated, and his face just seemed to sparkle. Listening to him, I had no doubt that his constant visualization and imagery as a youth contributed greatly to his success as an adult. He was a world champion years before he made his first jump. He had motivated and inspired himself by living in a world of make-believe. Only for Pete it wasn't make-believe— it was training.

In the words of an anonymous Apache shaman, *"We can only be what we give ourselves the power to be."* If I want to be a world-class anything I need to begin acting as if I already am. I need to see and experience this achievement repeatedly in my mind. Just like a child pretending to be a doctor, firefighter, police officer, or Olympic athlete, I need to pretend as if I am already there and "fake it 'til I make it." I need to intensify my dreaming and risk the possibility of disappointment.

A few months ago I woke up in the middle of the night

with a feeling of intense anxiety over some major personal risks I was taking in my life. I found myself just lying in bed, staring up at the ceiling, my mind filled with pictures of my dreams destroyed and my life in ruins. In a moment of fear I thought, "What if the roof caves in? What if I fail and all my plans fall to pieces?" And after what seemed like an eternity, a calm voice inside of me said, "Then you'll start over again. You've done it before and you can do it again." It was really that simple. Not necessarily easy, and it would certainly take some effort, but the concept was simple. If everything fell to pieces I could just "pick myself up, dust myself off, and start all over again" as the song says. Instantly the fear subsided, because I knew it was true, and I knew I could do it. I also knew that the fear could reappear at any moment and I'd have to deal with it all over again. But more than anything, I felt my commitment and resolve to confront it head on if it did return. The calm voice was right. I can start all over if I have to. I only have to begin by visualizing my new dream coming true.

I Own My Thoughts And Feelings

I feel victimized by the thoughts going on in my mind. Feelings, images, pictures, and sensations seem to flow in and out of my head with no rhyme or reason. They come and go all day long. I feel like I can't control the bad ones, and the good ones don't stay as long as I'd like. I try to hold on to them and figure out how they got there so I can make them reappear at will, but they always leave too soon and get replaced by the "bad stuff." These wretched thoughts are like unwanted company, like visitors who come unannounced. They just seem to muscle their way into my mind and stay as long as they want. They don't listen when I politely ask them to go, and when I beg them to leave they stay even longer, seemingly out of spite. I'm convinced they get a kick out of tormenting me all day long. What did I do to deserve this?

Sound familiar?   The eminent physicist David Bohm said, "Thought creates the world and then says 'I didn't do it.'" But the truth is that every thought, image, and picture in your mind is your creation. No one else put it there. If there's a movie playing in your head, you turned it on.

There's an expression, "No victims, only volunteers." We invite our thoughts, and if they stay it's because we allow them to. We may even protest their arrival at times, but in fact we are responsible for them.   We're continually making decisions about which ones will stay and which ones will go. The mind is our viewing screen and we own the channel selector. We can choose to use it or not. "Yes" and "No" are complete sentences that we can say to any thought at any time. Most of us however, don't realize this.

> I don't like some of these thoughts that I'm having. Why would I put them there in the first place, and even worse, why would I allow them to stay when they feel so bad? It must be that I have no control over them. And even if I did, what does this have to do with peak performance anyway?

Everything!

Peak performance in sport, as well as anywhere else in life, is achieved through a combination of relaxed attention and a high degree of control over the physical and mental aspects of the activity you're engaged in. In any sport, to function as if you're powerless over your thoughts and feelings is the equivalent of athletic suicide. To believe that your thinking is haphazard and beyond your control leaves you emotionally handicapped and at the mercy of your feelings, since feelings are the direct result of thoughts.

You've seen the results of this countless times. An umpire makes a questionable call in a tennis match and the player gets angry. The anger leads to a loss of focus as well as the next few points. A basketball player gets upset with himself after missing an easy shot. His self-criticism creates distraction and prevents him from clearing that shot from his mind. Consequently, he misses the next shot.

While athletes are as human as anyone else, these errors can be avoided with the skillful use of mental training techniques. Recall the awareness exercise on pages 8-9. When you think of a happy event you feel happy. When you think of a sad event you feel sad. This is basic cause and effect; a feeling is always a direct result of a thought. Mental training teaches how to change the thought and consequently the feeling, even if only for a short period of time—say for the duration of the event. The absence of these skills leaves you helpless with no control over stress, distraction, anger, fear, joy, arousal, etc. Without the ability to at least temporarily control your thoughts and emotions, all you can do is hope and pray that negative thinking doesn't appear during competition, because if it does, you're doomed.

CHAPTER 3

Let the Training Begin

You can map out a fight plan or a life plan, but when the action starts, it may not go the way you planned, and you're down to your reflexes—which means your training. That's where your roadwork shows. If you've cheated on that in the dark of morning—well, you're getting found out now, under the bright lights.
Joe Frazier

Training of any kind must have three components in order to be successful:

- A goal
- A plan to reach the goal
- A commitment to follow the plan

The Goal

A road map is of little value unless you know your destination. For most people, in fact, the difficulty is not in achieving goals but in setting them. To formulate a realistic goal two questions need to be asked: "What do I want to accomplish?" and "How will I know when I've accomplished it?" While this may sound overly simplistic, most people go astray at precisely this point. Their goal is too general and undefined, and consequently they have a difficult time creating a plan to reach it.

A goal needs to be *clear, specific, and measurable.* If your goal was to make a lot of money, you would first have to determine an amount before you could figure out a way to make it. If the amount you arrived at was $75,000 a year, for instance, that would be clear, specific and measurable. You would know by your accounting if your plan was working, if your goal had been reached, or how far you still had to go. You would also be able to make necessary adjustments or modifications to the plan to get back on track.

Let's say your goal is to be a really good skydiver. To design your training you must first decide what being a "really good skydiver" looks like to you. The term as it stands is vague and provides little information about the direction your training should take because being a "really good skydiver" means different things to different people. So you would have to begin by creating some specific, measurable criteria. For instance, you might consider yourself really good if you were able to do one or more of the following:

- Fall flat and stable and perform tight center turns, outfacing moves, side slides, forward/backward and up/down movements.
- Get invited on large formation loads.
- Perform a certain number of points in time.
- Participate on a competitive team.
- Enter and maintain a head down or sit fly position, etc.

A second way to formulate a goal is through visualization. Pretend you're a movie director and create a scene that depicts your goal being accomplished. What does that scene look like? How does the script read? What specifically are you doing in the movie that demonstrates your goal being achieved?

Regardless of the method, don't rush this process. The success of your training program rests entirely on the clarity of your goal, so spend as much time as you need answering your goal-defining questions. My own method of goal setting usually takes three to five drafts before I have a crystal-clear objective in mind.

I begin by sitting down and visualizing a general picture of what I wish to accomplish and then writing down everything that comes to mind. This process works best if it goes uncensored at first. I "free associate" and list my thoughts no matter how simple or absurd they may sound. At this stage I don't evaluate whether a thought is appropriate or not—I just write it down. Once the thoughts stop coming, I examine my list and keep any ideas that are clear, specific, and measurable. I eliminate everything else. I then write the list over and review it every day for about a week, adding and deleting ideas as I go. If a new thought comes to mind I put it down. If something doesn't seem to fit, I delete it. I revise until it looks and feels just right. If doubts persist, I share my list with friends to get their opinions. Once I arrive at an ambitious but realistic goal—one that I feel passionately about—I move on to the next step and design a plan to make it happen.

The Plan

Keep the plan as simple as possible. Decide what specific actions you need to take to achieve your goal, and determine their order of importance. Be practical and don't demand an investment or level of effort that is unreasonable or can't be maintained. Most diets and physical fitness programs self-destruct here due to unrealistic expectations that result in fatigue, burnout, or disgust. Human beings are strange animals. We either do little or nothing to reach our goals, or we create overly ambitious programs and fail to follow through. The result in either case is that we get nowhere.

I once heard a motivational speaker talk about the hundreds of thousands of home exercise machines sold each year that become dust collectors or clothing racks after a month or so. He said that we buy them with the best of intentions and then commit to an unrealistic training schedule.

We begin full steam with promises of daily exercise, and within a few weeks our training regimen is down to nearly nothing.   As we fail to live up to our high expectations we become discouraged and disappointed.   Self-disgust sets in; it's just one more time that we let ourselves down and failed to follow through on a plan. Paradoxically, instead of increasing our efforts to succeed, we begin to do less and less and eventually give up.

His solution to this problem is to create exercise plans that are ridiculously simple and require little to no effort.   Instead of making a major commitment, make an easy one that you can reach with no difficulty.   Work out five minutes a day, three days a week.   Anyone can do that.   It's enough to make you laugh, but not too much to make you fail.   And probably after five minutes of exercise you'll want to do more because it feels good.   And the more it feels good the more you'll want to do. You'll become successful at exercising, and this feeling will reinforce itself.

While I don't necessarily suggest this approach to most of my clients, the point made is valuable. My experience with peak performance training at all levels is that many of us tend to set unrealistic goals and take on more than we can handle. In our rush for success we make extravagant promises and commitments to training that require an effort above and beyond our ability, investment, or motivation level.

So take care to construct a plan that's realistic by continually asking yourself if it matches your commitment and level of motivation.   It needs to be practical for you at this time in your life.   If you can see yourself still doing it in two months, you probably have a good plan.   If you can't, make modifications now to avoid failure in the future.   Either decrease the intensity of the plan or make alterations in your life to accommodate the regimen you've created. As a rule of thumb it's always better to start conservatively and build from there. And remember— keep it simple.

The Commitment

Once the plan has been constructed, what remains is to follow through with every resource available to you. If your goal is extremely important, then nothing (barring a tragedy or crisis of major proportions) should get in your way. Never allow your changing moods to alter your plan. When you don't "feel" like working your plan, work it anyway. You need to be firm and unyielding in your commitment. Remember: you created this plan, and for good reason. It's designed to take you to your goal. If your goal is of minor importance, your plan should reflect this and not be too demanding. If it's of major importance, then there are very few things that should get in your way.

Once we put our plan into action, many of us, either consciously or unconsciously, begin to look for shortcuts. We search for easier/softer ways to accomplish our task. We may begin with a fierce determination, but as we get tired, bored, or outside our physical or psychological comfort level, we start to re-evaluate our program and cut corners. This is especially true in mental training because it often disturbs our equilibrium by taking us into uncharted territory. Most of us aren't used to these techniques and prefer to return to more familiar methods. We start finding reasons to modify our training and begin making excuses for not completing assignments.

Keep in mind that the plan is *your* vehicle to reach *your* goal. Therein lies its value and power. The goal is the prize— the thing of value. The plan is simply your method to attain it and may not be a whole lot of fun at times. It might sometimes seem dull, monotonous, exhausting, annoying, or discouraging. Occasionally, it may feel like a total waste of time. "Little voices" in your head might start telling you that it's just not worth all the effort, that you're expending far too much energy, that this is not as important as you once thought it was, that regardless of how hard you try you'll never reach it anyway so why continue. . . and so on.   It's your job to squelch those voices and stick with your plan.

Humans hate to feel discomfort for extended periods, especially mental discomfort, and go to extreme measures to avoid it. If you doubt what I'm saying take a look at your own life to see how many times you've given up on a goal, or a dream, or the pursuit of a relationship, hobby, career, etc. Be honest.   How often have you quit because things got too uncomfortable or the outcome became too uncertain? I'm not necessarily referring to physical discomfort. For most of us, emotional and mental discomfort are far more difficult to bear than any physical pain.

I know lots of superb athletes who can't tolerate the thought of having to meditate or sit quietly and do nothing. They'll do anything to avoid being still or getting in touch with their feelings and emotions.   They'd rather be involved in torturous physical exertion than experience the effects of silence. Give them something else, anything else, to do. Fix a car, paint a wall, fold the laundry, even wash the dishes, but NOT the dreaded mental training.

PEAK PERFORMANCE

IS	IS NOT
COMMITMENT	MOODS
GOALS	DESIRES
PASSION	WANTS
VISION	THOUGHTS
DISCIPLINE	CRAVINGS
CONVICTION	WHIMS

CHAPTER 4

The Tools

Anything worth doing is worth doing poorly at first.

Training Assessment Inventory

A chart for evaluating your performance strengths and weaknesses concerning specific skills, traits, attributes, and personality characteristics.

Action Plan

Part 1:   A comprehensive assessment and evaluation of significantly low scoring areas on the Training Assessment Inventory.

Part 2: Guidelines for designing and implementing a practical plan of action to improve those areas of weakness addressed in Part 1.

Please read the entire chapter before you proceed.

TRAINING ASSESSMENT INVENTORY

Rank each item as it applies to you on a scale from 1-5.
Ask yourself, "Am I weak in this area or strong?"
1=Very weak, 5=Very strong.
Items with an asterisk * are explained on the following page.

_____COMMITMENT TO GOAL
_____INTENSITY OF MOTIVATION
_____ABILITY TO MAINTAIN CONSISTENT MOTIVATION
_____LEVEL OF ENJOYMENT (IS SKYDIVING STILL FUN?)
_____COMPETITIVE ENERGY AND DRIVE
_____ABILITY TO COLLECT POSITIVE EXPERIENCES*
_____SPIRITUAL FITNESS*
_____ABILITY TO CONTROL DISTRACTION
_____ABILITY TO PERFORM UNDER PRESSURE
_____ABILITY TO MAINTAIN FOCUS
_____ABILITY TO TOLERATE DISCOMFORT
_____ABILITY TO CONTROL AROUSAL LEVELS
_____OPENNESS TO RECEIVING COACHING
_____CURRENT LEVEL OF SELF-CONFIDENCE
_____OPENNESS TO NEW IDEAS
_____ACTING ABILITY*
_____CURRENT LEVEL OF SELF-ESTEEM
_____SELF-ASSESSMENT SKILLS*
_____LEVEL OF TENACITY AND PERSEVERANCE
_____GENEROSITY TOWARD TEAMMATES
_____WILLINGNESS TO ACCEPT CRITICISM FROM OTHERS
_____DEGREE OF SELF-DISCIPLINE
_____PASSIONATE ABOUT GOALS
_____ABILITY TO MANAGE HABITS*
_____WILLINGNESS TO ACCEPT RESPONSIBILITY*
_____PHYSICAL CONDITIONING
_____SUCCESS COMFORT LEVEL*
_____INVESTMENT IN TEAM GOALS
_____SUPPORTIVE OF TEAMMATES
_____LEADERSHIP ABILITIES
_____ABILITY TO ENVISION PERSONAL GREATNESS*
_____EMOTIONAL FLEXIBILITY AND RESILIENCE*
_____MOOD CONSISTENCY

*Ability to Collect Positive Experiences. Do you tend to remember and carry your positive or your negative life experiences with you, skydiving or otherwise? A high score indicates your focus on the positive.

*Spiritual fitness. Does skydiving have meaning for you on a spiritual level? If not, leave this answer blank. If it does, score this category by indicating if your spiritual practice is presently strong or weak.

*Acting ability. In training and competing are you able to remain positive and "act as if" everything is going well in your life and your skydiving even when it is not?

*Self-assessment skills. When your performance is below par are you able to identify the cause of the problem?

*Ability to manage habits. To what degree do any habits or compulsive behaviors interfere with your performance?

*Willingness to accept responsibility. When things go wrong are you open to the possibility that you may have caused or contributed to the problem, or do you generally get defensive, make excuses, or blame someone or something outside of yourself?

*Success comfort level. Are you uneasy or uncomfortable in any way (think about it…) with success? If so, give yourself a low score.

*Ability to envision personal greatness. Can you truly imagine reaching your highest goal? Do you see it as a real possibility or as something you just hope will come true?

*Emotional flexibility and resilience. How well do you bounce back emotionally from major upsets and disappointments?

How To Use This Inventory

The TAI is a guide to assist you in evaluating yourself mentally and psychologically regarding your skydiving performance. This is not an opportunity to look good or impress anyone with high scores. Its aim is twofold—first, to provide you with a realistic appraisal and overview of your current strengths and weaknesses, and second, to target areas for immediate improvement.

Make some copies of the TAI before you write on it, then score yourself in each area on a scale from one to five. A five indicates that you possess the described trait to a high degree (think of a five as giving yourself an "A"), while a one indicates major weakness in that area (equivalent to an "F").

Get input from others

With your blank copies of the TAI, have one or more trusted friends or teammates also score you. You can then compare their assessment with yours and note any discrepancies.

We all have limited vision when it comes to evaluating ourselves, especially concerning mental and psychological traits. Over the years I have seen many extremely talented people fall short of their goals due to a lack of self-awareness. Most were very capable intelligent men and women who simply couldn't see what their friends, associates, and competitors could see so clearly. They believed they knew themselves and had no idea that their self-perception was impaired. They were aware of some areas where they needed to improve but clearly couldn't see some others.

Outside input gives us access to valuable information that we don't have on our own. Friends, coaches, teammates, spouses, and even our competitors view us from a perspective that we don't have. Consequently, these people often have a more accurate picture of our abilities than we do. Their contribution is invaluable and we should definitely ask for it.

If you're uncomfortable with having someone assess your abilities because you fear that they may be overly harsh in their criticism, remember that this is entirely for your benefit. A thorough and accurate TAI supports your commitment to your goal. If someone's evaluation of you is harsh, so be it, as long as it represents the truth. The truth is what you are searching for, not an ego stroking. The more accurate the assessment, the more effectively you can design an improvement plan to overcome any weakness and enhance your performance. So put your pride away and allow others to tell you what they really think. (Sometimes the best person for the job is the person you least want to ask.)

Keep in mind that the TAI is not a test or an assessment of your value as a human being, nor is it designed to inflate your ego with great scores. Its sole purpose is to uncover obstacles to peak performance, and everybody has them. In fact, most of us have more than we realize.

For example, if you believe you are teachable and coachable but your teammates see you as closed minded and resistant to change, then this needs to be brought to your attention. Similarly, you may be unaware that certain behaviors, attitudes, or aspects of your lifestyle are limiting your overall performance. The bottom line is this: *If you are 100% committed to achieving your goal, then nothing short of brutal self-honesty will do.* You must be willing to look under every rock, stone, and pebble to uncover anything that may be getting in your way. You must have the courage to see yourself "as you are today" in order to transform yourself into "who you want to be tomorrow." Anything less will keep you from reaching your goals.

Over the years I have identified two major perceptual impairments that consistently damage performance. Both are insidious, both are universal (we all have them,) and both are preventable as long as we use others to assist us in evaluating ourselves. These impairments are blindspots and denial.

Blindspots are things that are outside of or obscured from our vision or things about which we are simply unaware. We think we see everything, but in reality we do not. For instance, we are driving into the sun and don't realize the extent to which the glare is limiting our ability to see oncoming traffic until we impact another vehicle. Up to that point we believed our sight picture was accurate. The resulting accident tells us differently. Another example is looking but not seeing a canopy below us— maybe because it's blending in with the terrain or maybe because we just missed it as we visually scanned the area. If we're lucky we notice it before it's too late, if not we're in trouble. In both examples, we are motivated, attentive, and conscientious, but these attributes are not enough to prevent problems. Think about how many times you've seen a video of yourself skydiving and realized only then that you were doing something you were totally unaware of, or how many times you missed seeing something in a skydive that was right in front of your eyes. These are blindspots. Without the benefit of outside help (in this case the video) these problems usually go undetected.

Denial on the other hand is the act of *unconsciously choosing* to hide something from ourselves that has already entered our awareness. In denial we begin by seeing or experiencing something uncomfortable—judge it to be unacceptable for some reason—and then instantly eliminate it from our consciousness before it has a chance to take hold. These are usually behaviors or personality and character traits that we are resistant to change, or qualities in ourselves that we subconsciously find repulsive or reproachable. Through some clever trick of the mind we either rationalize the awareness out of existence or negate it entirely like an ostrich putting its head in the sand. Unconsciously we believe that this awareness is emotionally dangerous and will hurt us in some way. We may feel that we need this trait or behavior in order to survive, or fear that we could not change it even if we wanted to.

An interesting thing about denial is that we do not recognize it in ourselves. Our denial doesn't allow it. The twisted logic goes something like this: if it doesn't exist I don't have to face it; if I don't have to face it, I won't have to fail at trying to change it. The tragedy is that denial prevents us from dealing with those issues, which once resolved, would clear the path toward our goal.

The difference between a blindspot and denial is that in a blindspot you never even see the problem; it never enters your awareness. In denial, however, the problem momentarily enters your awareness but is immediately erased or suppressed. Consequently, denial is much more insidious and damaging to performance. Blocking awareness requires constant vigilance and the expenditure of a great deal of energy to maintain the illusion that everything is okay when it is not. Over time this requires that more and more bits of reality be suppressed to preserve the self-deception. The longer the denial continues the more isolated and insulated you become from reality. Often the people around you know exactly what is being denied and what it is costing you. They must choose between supporting your dysfunction by remaining quiet or confronting you and risking your anger and rejection.

Compare assessments

The next step is to compare your TAI scores with the scores given to you by others. Discuss any major discrepancies with the people involved in an attempt to reach some consensus, especially in your weakest areas. If agreement is not reached, remember that in the final analysis it is your assessment that is most important. That is the one your Action Plan will be based on.

For Teams: One option is to have each member share their scores at a team meeting and get feedback from other members. Done in a supportive context, this can be a powerful individual learning experience as well as a dynamic team-building exercise. However, a note of caution—a team must be in a relatively healthy place emotionally and have already established a strong foundation of trust for this degree of sensitive communication to be successful. This is an opportunity to authentically share and further strengthen the team's bonds. This exercise is not an excuse to bash a teammate for something that has been bothering you all year. Those kinds of negative feelings need to be appropriately expressed at a Communication Meeting. (See Chapter 7, Team Communication, page 68.)

Combining categories

Although each category on the TAI is separate and distinct and measures a specific skill or ability, some have features that overlap. Examine your low scores and note if any of them are in related categories or follow a pattern. If so, it may be possible to combine them into one Action Plan. For example, while the 'ability to control distraction' and the 'ability to maintain focus' are two distinct categories, they do overlap in some respects and can be treated as one issue. The same can be said of 'intensity of motivation' and 'ability to maintain consistent motivation,' 'openness to receiving coaching' and 'openness to new ideas,' and areas that involve team skills such as 'investment in team goals' and 'supportive of teammates.' (Note that the primary purpose in combining categories is to help reduce the number of targeted areas to no more than three. If you only have three low scoring areas to begin with, then combining is optional.)

It is also important to note that not all areas on the TAI are of equal importance regarding their impact on performance and goal achievement.   For instance, a score of three on 'commitment to goal' can be much more damaging over time than a lower score on 'ability to control arousal levels.' The reason is because low arousal scores will affect only certain areas of performance, whereas low commitment scores can negatively impact every area.   Similarly, low scores in areas that involve motivation, energy, enjoyment, passion, self-discipline, and habit management are capable of severely undermining your efforts to reach your goal. These areas need to be addressed first.

I strongly suggest focusing on no more than three areas at any given time. Less than three is okay, but more than that may create an overload or dilute your efforts to the point of ineffectiveness. An exception to this rule could apply if working with a coach who agreed with your decision to take on additional areas. But if in doubt, keep it simple.

ACTION PLAN

Part One—History and Background

1. Identify the problem area revealed by the TAI as clearly and specifically as you can, and answer the following questions.
2. When did you first become aware of this problem?
3. What is its origin? Do you know how or why it began?
4. In previous efforts to improve it, what did or didn't work?
5. Is there anything in your past that needs to be addressed or resolved to enable you to improve this area?
6. What does this problem cost you? How does it currently impact your life mentally, physically, emotionally and spiritually, both in and out of skydiving? Be specific.
7. Are there secondary gains you derive by not eliminating the problem? Think carefully; be honest.
8. Are you willing to make a commitment to forgo these secondary gains in order to improve this area?
9. If this problem ceased to exist, what new possibilities would open up for you?

Part Two—Designing the Plan

1. The plan should include changes in your behavior and thinking.
   Behavior:
   - What will you *do* differently? What new behaviors will you begin to experiment with?
   - What will you *say* differently (to yourself and others)?
   Thinking:
   - What will you *see* differently (in your thoughts and imagination)?
   - What will you *choose to believe* differently?
2. Changes should be stated in positive terms rather than negative ones. For instance, "I will eat nutritiously," as

compared to "I will not eat junk food," or "I will visualize myself on a winning team," as compared to "I will stop my negative thinking about my skydiving."

3. Be concrete and specific. For instance, list the kinds of nutritious foods you will eat. Create a detailed visualization of what a winning team looks like for you.

4. Read your plan over and ask yourself if your goals are realistic and achievable. If the answer is no, revise it now.

5. Sign and date your plan.

6. (Optional) Have a close friend or teammate also sign your plan.

You can begin designing your Action Plan once you have targeted your areas for improvement. Do not cheat yourself at this point by just reading the outline and only thinking about the answers. Actually sit down and write them out, even if you hate to write. The time spent will be well worth it. The act of writing, in and of itself, creates change. It is not just an activity on the way to change—it is change. In addition, writing allows you to see the details and hidden aspects of your particular issue, especially the part you played in creating it and the way your thinking and behavior have kept it alive. If you are completely honest with yourself in doing this work, you will probably find that your greatest obstacle to peak performance is nothing other than yourself. Depending on your willingness and level of commitment, this newfound insight can open up enormous possibilities. The choice is yours.

Part one of the Action Plan is about gaining a thorough understanding of the origin and nature of the area to be improved. This information provides the foundation for the plan's creation. It does not matter if you answer the questions one at a time or do it in narrative form. The point is to answer all of the questions before moving on to part two where you will actually design your plan. While most of these questions are self-explanatory, there are some that require further clarification.

Question 5: *Is there anything in your past that needs to be addressed or resolved in order for you to improve this area?*
Oftentimes problems in the present are a direct result of unfinished situations from the past. An athlete I once coached scored low on 'level of enjoyment,' 'ability to control distraction' and 'ability to maintain focus.' In writing part one of his action plan it became evident that he had developed a strong resentment toward two of his teammates over an incident from the previous year. He felt justified in his ill feelings and had no intention of changing them. However, as his resentment grew over time (as resentments always do), he became increasingly annoyed and frustrated and more easily distracted during training. Eventually his performance deteriorated. The fact that his feelings were justified no longer mattered. His resentments were now interfering with his goals and he was willing to consider a change. In creating his Action Plan he agreed to sit down with his teammates and discuss his feelings openly in order to resolve this conflict.

Two additional areas of difficulty that frequently have origins in the past are negative thinking and low self-esteem. These problems are often the result of negative childhood experiences and exposure to faulty or misguided child-rearing methods. Our outlook, attitudes, inner dialogue, and self-image frequently reflect how we were raised and what we were taught as children. This does not mean that we get to blame our parents and teachers for our current problems, but simply that we acknowledge that we may have carried old values and behaviors into our present lives without evaluating their validity or effectiveness. Along these lines, an Action Plan might require a thorough exploration and assessment of past experiences for the purpose of designing specific positive re-programming techniques. Contrary to what it might seem, this is not a particularly difficult task although it does require time, effort, and honesty.

Question 7: *Are there secondary gains you derive by not addressing the problem?*
Most negative thoughts and behaviors have a hidden dividend—a secondary gain attached to them that motivates us to keep them alive and operational. This applies to even the most destructive ones that we may be trying to get rid of. To the outside observer these thoughts and behaviors may appear to be totally dysfunctional and without value, but upon closer examination we often uncover another purpose—a secret payoff.

All behaviors exist for a good reason whether we know that reason or not. Human beings are not stupid regardless of how it may look at times. We think logically and have an instinct to survive and avoid pain. We behave in certain ways because we believe these behaviors serve us.

Our fears, for instance, while they may often seem irrational and unreasonable, are designed by our minds to protect us from getting hurt. Whether that hurt is real or imagined doesn't matter. Whether that hurt is only a memory of the past and will never again occur in the future also doesn't matter. Fear is often the mind's way of informing us of the worst possible scenario in a situation in order to prepare us for that eventuality. It is simply running on automatic and doing its job. It doesn't care that the danger may be long gone, never to return.

So in answering question seven, look for the secondary gain in the negative thoughts or behaviors you are trying to change. For instance, while a harbored resentment may make you angry and uncomfortable, it also protects you. It keeps you at an emotionally safe distance from the person who hurt you so they won't be able to hurt you again. That's a secondary gain—a payoff. You just have to decide if it's worth the price.

Performance anxiety is another good example of a negative behavior with a secondary gain. It occurs when two fundamental beliefs are fused together. The first is, "mistakes are emotionally dangerous and painful and need to be avoided at all cost," and the second is, "worrying helps us to avoid making mistakes." When you combine the two the result is performance anxiety. In a sense, you make yourself "worry" because you believe it will help you avoid the pain of failure. As with resentment, the payoff is psychological safety, but the cost is high.

Even negative thinking and low self-esteem have secondary gains, although you might be hard pressed to admit that at the time. Negative thinking, for instance, prepares you for failure by reducing the distance you will have to fall if you do not succeed. It allows you to rehearse failure over and over again in your mind so that you are ready for it when it comes. The problem is that this continued rehearsal helps you to create the very thing that you are trying to avoid.

The same is true for low self-esteem. At the risk of oversimplifying, low self-esteem is simply a continuous flow of negative inner dialogue accompanied by vivid images of failure. You are picturing the worst in your mind while you are telling yourself, "I can't do it," "I'm not good enough," "If I try I'll just fail anyway," and "Even if I succeed this time I probably won't succeed next time," etc.

So what could possibly be the payoff in all of this? You guessed it—safety, security, comfort. If you assume you are going to fail, then you don't have to do much or risk much. You can guarantee your security and maintain a reasonable level of comfort by not extending yourself too far. But sadly, you will never know the wonder and excitement of living on the edge as you reach for the highest of your dreams. As a friend of mine often says, "If you want to do anything worthwhile, you have to go out on the skinny branches."

Assessing your improvement

Once you design your Action Plan, all that remains is to follow it on a daily basis and monitor your progress. This can be done informally by reading your plan every day or so, noticing if you are taking the actions you have decided to take, and observing whether or not there has been any improvement in the targeted area.

For those who prefer more structure, I suggest getting a small notebook and numbering the pages from one to thirty. If you have more than one Action Plan, create a column for each plan on every page. At the end of each day write brief notes indicating the actions you have taken and whether or not they have worked. At the end of the first week evaluate your plan's overall effectiveness. If by the end of the second week you have been taking all the required actions and still see no improvement in the targeted area, consider making some changes in your plan.

Generally speaking, if you consistently and faithfully follow your plan, you will experience significant improvement within a month.

Remember that you do not have to be on the drop zone to improve any of these areas. You will have opportunities each day to practice new behaviors and ways of thinking whether you are skydiving or not. Although skydiving may have initially provided the motivation for you to work on these areas, the reason you are experiencing difficulty to begin with is probably because you have unrecognized dysfunctional behaviors or beliefs restricting you. With no exception, every area on the TAI can be improved by using events and circumstances in your daily life as opportunities for growth and change.

You are not required to improve every shortcoming you become aware of, but you need to recognize that there are consequences for allowing a dysfunctional or non-productive mental behavior to continue. It is okay to say "Right now I don't want to work on this" or "Right now I'm too uncomfortable changing this part of me." But it is mentally dangerous to say, "I'll *never* change this," or "I *can't* change that," or worst of all, "I've tried to change this before and I've proven to myself that I just can't do it." These negative statements are setups for failure and should not be tolerated for even one second, especially by someone with a vision—(that's you)—reaching for a goal. Besides, they are all lies anyway. You can never know what you will be capable of in the next moment.

We have all seen incredible examples of transformation in our own lives as well as in the lives of others. We have seen people who have overcome seemingly insurmountable obstacles because they had a dream and were determined to see it through. Nothing could get in their way for long. They maintained a positive focus and refused to believe the internal defeatist voice that told them to quit.

Make no mistake about it, everybody hears that voice on occasion—even the best of us. Read the life story of any great individual, past or present, and you will find they heard it too. Sometimes it is so loud that we consider listening to it. But if we can endure for a while—even a short time—we find that *the voice goes away.* It may come back occasionally to see if we are interested, but if we are determined not to listen to it, it goes away again. And each time it goes away, it stays away longer.

Do not think that champions achieve greatness because they are exempt from negative thinking. They are not. They just learn to expect it and deal with it immediately rather than allow it to get a foothold. They practice discounting it and redirecting their focus rather than fighting negativity. They know that *feelings aren't facts and thoughts aren't reality.* And because they are determined to reach their goals, they are selective about the thoughts they are willing to entertain.

CHAPTER 5

The Miracle Tool

*The important thing is this:
to be ready at any moment to sacrifice
what you are for what you might become.*
Charles Dubois

More than any other single tool or technique, the Personal Vision Statement is the most powerful peak performance instrument available. When used correctly, this document generates the motivation necessary to bring about extraordinary change by keeping you continually focused on your goal and the steps necessary to achieve it. But most of all, it's a direct link to the driving force behind your goal—your passion and enthusiasm—your deepest reasons for being on this path.

Designing Your Vision Statement

1. The goal

Write a clear, simple description of your goal in first person, present tense as if it has already been accomplished. Use terms such as "I am..." or "I have..." as compared to "I want...," "I am going to...," or "I will...." For instance, instead of saying "I want a gold medal in..." or "I hope to win a gold medal in...," say, "I have a gold medal in..." or

"I am a gold medal winner in...." State the goal as if it has been achieved. Begin thinking, living, and acting as if you already have what you are striving for.

Every time we visualize or "dirt dive" a skydive we're utilizing this mental principle. We're thinking, living, and acting as if we've already executed a perfect skydive. We're allowing ourselves to experience the goal *before* it happens. Then we can achieve it because we've already been there.

2. Timeframe for the goal

Decide on a completion date. Ask yourself, "When will I achieve this goal?" Place it at the top of your statement. It may be ambitious, but it must be realistic.

3. Your plan to achieve it

List the steps necessary to achieve your goal. Be concrete and specific. These steps can be physical, mental, emotional, and spiritual. They should include what you will say, do, think, believe, etc. As with your goal, list them in the first person, present tense. For instance, "I work out at the gym three times a week and do yoga twice a week." "I train hard with my team every weekend." "I get a good night's sleep and refrain from partying before every training day." "I spend ten minutes a day visualizing myself winning a medal at the Nationals." You don't have to list every minute aspect of your plan, but the main parts should be there.

4. Why the goal is important

What makes this goal have value or meaning for you? What about it do you find exciting, moving, thrilling, fulfilling, rewarding, or spiritually significant? Find your most passionate reasons.

The more important and meaningful the goal, the greater your chances of achieving it. When you're bored, tired, or just not in the mood to follow your plan on any given day, reading this section of your vision statement can re-connect you with your passion and enthusiasm—your deepest and most compelling reasons for being on this journey to begin with.

If your reasons lack depth and intensity, then this will be reflected in reduced drive and determination, especially when the going gets tough. Similarly, if you're unemotional about your goal, your motivation will also be weak and inconsistent.

The key to following through on any training plan, especially one that requires sustained effort over time, is to fully experience your passion and excitement for your goal as often as possible. Nothing less will do.

5. Instructions for use

Once you've completed your statement, make a number of copies and place them in areas where you will see it frequently such as your car, bathroom, wallet, daily planner, log book, etc. Read your Vision Statement as often as you can, at least once in the morning and once at bedtime. Read it with feeling, purpose and commitment, as if your life depends on it—it does.

Daily readings keep you focused on your goals in addition to preparing you for their arrival. *I can not overstate the importance of this practice*; its value is beyond words. I've used it personally and professionally for years and have seen incredible results time and time again. Consistency and perseverance are the keys to success.

Olympic champion Lanny Bassham, who uses a similar technique called the Directive Affirmation, states that continued practice will yield one of two possible results. Either you'll reach your goal or you'll stop reading the statement. Nothing else is possible.

CHAPTER 6

Teamwork

*Don't aim at success—the more you aim at it and
make it a target, the more you are going to miss it.
For success, like happiness, cannot be pursued;
it must ensue...as the unintended side-effect of one's personal
dedication to a course greater than oneself.*
Viktor Frankl

Ultimately, at its deepest and finest, true teamwork
is a spiritual experience. I hope you will not leave
this book with the idea that true teamwork can be
generated by a bunch of techniques or gimmicks or
easy steps. Teamwork comes about only when we
are absolutely committed to the principles of
teamwork, to our teammates, and to our vision.
And I would take it a step further and say that the
deepest, richest, most meaningful, most intense
form of teamwork takes place when we are also
committed—body, mind, and spirit—to God.
(Williams, 225)

A Spiritual Experience

While I love the above quote by Pat Williams of the Orlando Magic, I debated about whether to include the last sentence out of concern that some would be "turned off" at the notion of connecting God with teamwork. I decided to let you decide; if it fits in your belief system, use it. If it doesn't, leave it out.

I'm not suggesting that you have to believe in God to be involved in true teamwork. Belief in a particular God or doctrine is not the issue. What I am suggesting is that spirituality and teamwork are closely interrelated as they both require action, commitment, relationship, and sharing in order to thrive. The vitality of any team is a direct result of how its members treat themselves and one another, their ability to give and receive, and their willingness to relate with compassion, authenticity, and understanding.

I know some kind, wonderful, generous people who don't think about "God" one way or the other. God is simply not in their vocabulary or belief system, although their spirituality and capacity to love are very obvious and present nonetheless. On the other hand, I know some very devout believers in God who are totally self-absorbed and out of touch with the needs of those around them. They're not bad people, they just seem to be isolated and disconnected and missing a fundamental sense of what teamwork is all about.

Years ago I watched a television special on the wonders of the human body. In one of the segments, they took a single heart cell and viewed it through a microscope where it could be seen to pulsate with a very definite rhythm. They then took another heart cell from a different person and placed it on the slide next to the first cell. As expected, both cells beat in very different rhythms. What happened next I will never forget. Suddenly, as if they were connected or joined in some mysterious way, they began beating together. They began beating as one. They had formed a team.

That experience for me exemplifies the magic and spirit of teamwork—the miracle that can occur when two or more very different and unique individuals agree to share a common ground in order to fulfill a vision that neither can do alone. Whether it's a family, a marriage, a friendship, a business group, or a sports team, genuine teamwork always demonstrates that the whole is much, much more than the sum of its parts. It is a reminder that two or more people joining together for a mutual purpose can and do create extraordinary things. In a sense, it is proof that teamwork doesn't require spirituality; it is spirituality.

A Complex Experience

Teamwork is a rich and delicate union that can be profoundly rewarding on one hand and highly stressful on the other. A feeling of intense satisfaction and fulfillment can rapidly be followed by one of anger and frustration as group dynamics fluctuate from moment to moment. I have found it to be one of the most complex emotional experiences a person can enjoy—or endure—depending on your attitude, viewpoint, and past experience. Some people love to be on teams—others hate it. Some appreciate the fellowship and sharing and enjoy being part of a larger whole. Others find it restricts their individuality and is entirely too demanding and unpredictable. When I think of teamwork the most descriptive word that comes to mind is "adventure," and that's an understatement.

What makes teamwork so emotionally charged is the absence of an "I" in the word team.

> *Once "I" become a member of a team, who "I" am and what "I" need becomes less important than who the "team" is and what the "team" needs.*

In practice this can be a tough principle to follow, but (like it or not) it's extremely effective. Not only does it get the job done, but it also creates fellowship and bonding. Many teams, however, operate in reverse. This is one reason teams have so many problems and fall apart so often and so quickly. People mistakenly join with the expectation that the team is there to fulfill their needs when the opposite is really the case. That's why it's important to carefully consider all that you'll be investing and committing to prior to "signing on the dotted line."

A "We" Experience

"There is no limit to what a man can do or where he can go if he doesn't mind who gets the credit" (Robert Woodruff, former president of the Coca-Cola Corporation).

A team is fundamentally a "we" experience and yet it's composed of individuals with their own personal goals and aspirations. The price of membership is an agreement to place the team's needs first and your needs second. This becomes problematic because of the nature of the ego—the needs of the "I".

This ego is probably the biggest reason for joining the team to begin with. It wants attention, recognition, and success and joins the team as a means to that end. And yes, we are all in this sport because we have noble motives and a healthy desire to fully express who we really are. There's no denying that. But there's also no denying that on another level we're self-centered and want everything our own way. And we certainly don't want anyone interfering with our designs for happiness and success. We have an agenda and we plan to see it through. And ego is determined to have two things: to win and to look good (but if we can't win, the least we can do is look good in the process.)

Once you join a team, the ego is forced to make adjustments. The first thing it learns (hopefully) is the value of remaining silent, because there are other strong egos around also trying to get their needs met. And we know that when egos compete with one other the result is noise, conflict, and chaos. When that happens the job never gets done, and the goal is never achieved. So the ego has a choice.

It can be demanding and insist on having its own way, or it can restrain itself and attend to the needs of the team in the belief that as the team grows—so will I; as the team's needs are met—so will mine. A healthy ego eventually finds a balance between the two. But in the beginning, to arrive at this balance, it must continually be reminded (by its owner) to be quiet and not "act out" when it doesn't get its way.

As ego learns patience, it begins to settle for silence in exchange for team identity and cohesion. It realizes that in order to achieve its objective it has to play the game a new way.

Once you join a team the rules that govern personal achievement change. You're forced to interact with others who have their own desires, expectations, and some very strong opinions about how to achieve them. You want what you want, they want what they want, and often the two don't meet. You also need their help to get what you want, and they need yours in return. Operating within this framework demands patience, compromise, and some very good communication skills. For most of us this requires a shift in both our thinking and behavior in ways that we are not accustomed to.

In order for you to get what you want you have to give it away first. I can't tell you how many times I've heard someone say about a teammate, "Well they're not doing their share so I'll be damned if I'll do mine." And yes, you will be (metaphorically speaking) if that's your attitude. In fact, the whole team will be damned to being miserable and ineffective. Everybody will be waiting for everybody else to make the next investment of effort before they become willing to make theirs. Anger and resentment will flourish with no productivity. The energy drain will be enormous, and for what? How many times have you seen this happen? Now be honest. How many times have you contributed to this happening?

If I want hard work from my teammates, I have to be willing to sweat first. If I want the security that comes from team cohesion and bonding, I have to make sure that I'm doing everything I can to make my teammates feel secure. If I want unconditional trust from the people I'm flying with, then I have to prove that I'm loyal and trustworthy first.   I have to demonstrate that I'll be there for you, even if you're not able to be there for me right now.   But if I'm waiting for you to contribute before I will, we're all in trouble.

This notion of "giving in advance of receiving" doesn't make sense to some people until they try it and see for themselves how productive it is. If you've ever been on a team that operates this way, you know how quickly it builds a foundation of trust and how easily things get accomplished once that foundation is in place. You also know that it takes effort to maintain, especially when you're exhausted and disappointed and things go wrong, and you feel like blaming someone for all the problems. But it's precisely in those moments that you have to keep reminding yourself why you joined the team to begin with.   You have to take a good hard look at your goals and dreams—hold them up close and feel how much they mean to you—and then put them aside and attend to the needs of your team.

This degree of fellowship and generosity is always present in successful and lasting relationships.   Instead of responding with distance, anger, and resentment to behaviors you don't like in others, you step back for a moment and strive to create in yourself an attitude of acceptance and tolerance. You don't attempt to be phony or inauthentic—you don't smile and stuff your feelings when you're furious, or pretend everything is okay when it's not. You honestly communicate your feelings and opinions as clearly as possible in a way that allows the other person to hear and understand what you're saying.

Suppressing or repressing your feelings only creates resentments later on. If you're disappointed, angry, or upset then by all means express it, but do so without blaming or finger pointing. If your emotions are charged, try sharing them with someone else prior to confronting the person you're upset with. This helps discharge the intensity of the feelings, enabling you to be reasonably calm and focused in the confrontation. If you're in "attack mode" chances are your message won't be heard, because attack usually terminates effective communication and evokes a reactive and defensive posture in the listener.

Positive expectation creates positive results. If you're serious about generating constructive change, it's important to convey a message that implies "While I don't necessarily like what happened or what you did, I trust your investment and commitment to this team, so I'm not going to judge you or reject you."

This attitude allows others the freedom to make mistakes and the space they need to make improvements. It creates an atmosphere of trust and support. It becomes an invitation to grow—not a demand to change. Furthermore, there's no reason for anyone to be defensive because no one is under attack. Most importantly, it compels and motivates others to work on the problem at hand because they know you believe in them and genuinely care. They also know you're waiting with positive expectancy and faith in their ability to change, and that they have a responsibility to you and the team to be the best they can possibly be.

Several years ago I worked with a team that was experiencing major internal conflict and struggling for its survival. In one particularly heated meeting, everyone was throwing complaints, accusations, and demands back and forth for over an hour. The room was filled with anger, frustration, and confusion. People were bouncing off each other's negative energy like pinballs. I was trying in vain to help them find a way to redirect this energy in a positive direction, but nothing I did seemed to make any difference. Throughout all of this one of the members had been conspicuously quiet. At one point someone turned to him and asked for his opinion. His response was sincere and without judgment. He said, "Right now my opinion doesn't matter. I'm not interested in being right. The last thing this meeting needs is another opinion."

I almost fell off my chair. Nothing I could have said would have been half as effective as that statement coming from a team member. In a few short sentences he shifted his team back on track by reminding them that their goals could only be achieved by putting the team first. His words had power because they reflected his actions. He "walked the walk" so to speak—he led by example. He seemed to know intuitively that the way to achieve his personal goal was to look outside of himself to the needs of his team.

He was right. The last thing his team needed at that meeting was another opinion, demand, complaint, or accusation. He chose to listen and be patient, which is what he wanted others to do. He was caring for himself by caring for his teammates. By attending to the needs of his team he was ultimately acting in the service of his own goals. Although he wasn't aware of it at the time, his response was based on having asked himself two important questions: "What does my team need at this point?" and "How can I meet that need?"

A Loving Experience

In my coaching I often encounter resistance to this notion of putting individual needs second to the needs of the team. People question why such a sacrifice should be necessary when their reason for joining the team to begin with is a personal one. They wonder how they can possibly reach their goal if they keep putting it second to someone else's.

Understanding how and why this process works requires a shift in perception—a reframing of the picture. When your right arm is broken and your left has to compensate, there's no sacrifice involved, and the right doesn't thank the left for all its help. There's a built-in understanding that they're in partnership working towards the same objective. When you stay awake all night to care for a sick child or friend or go out of your way to help someone in need, again there's not the slightest trace of sacrifice in either of these situations. Why? Because you consider these people teammates. You just define team differently for each group that you're involved with. Sometimes it's family, sometimes friends, and sometimes community. You know that by contributing toward the safety and happiness of your teammates you derive a sense of satisfaction and fulfillment and enhance the quality of your own life. You know that by helping your teammates reach their goals you move closer to your own. You become willing to give whatever is required because you know in your heart it's the right thing to do—you know in your mind it's the practical thing to do—and you know in your gut it's the only thing to do.

But you say:

> That's fine when it comes to my child, spouse or close friends, but what does this have to do with skydiving? I don't love my teammates. I don't even like some of them. We fly together and have some fun but it's just not the same thing. Why should I bend over backwards for someone who's not doing much of anything for me? Why should I let someone take advantage of me like that?

My answer is:

> You'd better love your teammates. Even if you
> don't like them you'd better love them on some
> level, or at least treat them as if you do, because
> you've given them a very special place in your
> life. Not only do you spend a significant amount
> of time with them in a sport that demands
> interdependence and fellowship, but you've also
> entrusted them with the responsibility of helping
> you make one of your dreams come true. That's
> a big deal and requires a major investment on
> everyone's part. A gesture of love nurtures and
> sustains that investment and helps to guarantee
> its success.

Now I'm not talking about love as an "emotion or sentiment,"
but rather love as an "action or behavior." This type of love can
be very functional and practical. In his book *Mental Health
Through Will Training,* Dr. Abraham Low states that there are
times when it is important to express warmth and caring even
when you don't feel it. He refers to this as "making an insincere
gesture of sincerity." He encourages his clients to behave, on
occasion, in a loving or positive manner even when they feel the
opposite, and to do so in order to "constructively" change the
outcome of a situation. For instance, when a young child shows
us a picture they drew, we often respond with an "insincere
gesture of sincerity" by saying all kinds of wonderful things
about it even though it may look grotesque and we don't have a
clue as to what it is. And if it's our own child's picture we'll go
so far as to display it prominently on the refrigerator.

Similarly, when the Dalai Lama was asked if he was
angry at China for invading his country, he replied that he
wasn't because additional anger would only worsen the
situation and therefore wouldn't be practical. He decided
instead to generate an action of love as a demonstration of his

good will and desire for positive change. He wasn't suppressing his feelings but rather transforming them into something functional—something that worked. *He was designing his behavior to be in line with his objectives* and using that as a yardstick to measure all of his actions. He was asking himself, *"Is my present course of action moving me toward my goal or away from it?"*

Now, we aren't Dalai Lamas, but if our goal is effective teamwork, each of us has to re-evaluate some of our existing attitudes and behaviors. We have to think ahead to our objective and design our communication to that end. On occasion we have to restrain our emotions and transform our hostile or combative feelings into ones that are compassionate, practical, and productive.

A Learning Experience

A number of years ago I was on a team with someone I really disliked. Everything about him annoyed me. Generally I'm an accepting and nonjudgmental person, but every time I saw this guy he seemed to press all of my buttons. In fact, I concluded that the planet would be better off without him because as far as I was concerned he had no socially redeeming value of any kind. I knew I had to find a way to neutralize the negative effect he was having on me because it was starting to make me miserable.

Looking back on this experience I'm grateful for how much it taught me. My first lesson was in realizing that I had a choice about how I reacted to him. Frankly, this awareness came as a big surprise to me at the time. Although I'm a fairly intelligent person, I had become convinced that I had no alternative but to feel anger and disgust in his presence. It never dawned on me that my reaction to him was my choice—that there were a variety of other possible reactions to choose from—and that no one was forcing me to dislike him or be annoyed by his behavior.

Slowly I began to see my unhappiness as my own creation, based on my attitudes, beliefs, and opinions. I could have ignored his behavior but had chosen not to do so. I could have stayed centered and focused on my own life but had decided to look at his instead. This mess was my doing based on my perceptions, interpretations and choices. The only power he had over me was the power I was giving him. He wasn't the cause of my misery—I was.

What a discovery! What a revelation to realize that I was in control—and what an enormous responsibility accompanied that revelation. *It wasn't him I needed to change, it was me.* I was allowing him to make me miserable. I was giving away my energy and my power. I was wasting my time talking about him, judging him, and complaining about him to anyone who'd listen. I was the one who was filled with resentment. And you know what they say; "Having a resentment is like peeing your pants. You're the only one who feels it."

My second lesson came from the advice of a good friend who suggested I write a list of this guy's good qualities. Initially I was repulsed by the idea and unwilling to admit to myself or anyone else that he even had any good qualities. But I accepted the challenge, knowing in my gut that my friend was right. And sure enough, I found some. Not a lot, but enough to allow me to begin seeing him in a different light.

I noticed that as I recognized his positive qualities and reacted to him differently, my struggle ended.

And interestingly enough, he also began to change.

Chapter 7

Team Communication

Who you are shouts so loudly that I can't hear what you're saying.
Ralph Waldo Emerson

A team is only as good as each member's ability to communicate effectively. Poor verbal communication on the ground will translate into poor non-verbal communication in the air. A team without solid communication skills may do well for a while but generally won't sustain any consistent level of performance over time. As challenges arise and personalities clash, as they do in every team, inadequate communication skills will be sorely manifested in weak problem solving abilities. As pressure mounts, team members will avoid situations that need attention and will attempt to remedy difficult problems with a quick fix whenever possible. They'll bypass important issues rather than work through them and eventually accumulate a string of unfinished situations, resentments, bruised egos, etc. They'll become problem-focused rather than solution-oriented. Before long they'll be competing against each other rather than against their opponents. Trust will vanish; anger, disgust, and fatigue will set in; goals will become blurred; gossip will increase along with blaming and complaining; members will start finding excuses to miss training; everybody will begin wishing they were on a different team, and the thrill of competition will vanish. Does this sound familiar?

The ongoing practice of open and honest communication is essential for any team that aspires to quality and longevity. Simply making an agreement to be candid with one another is nice, but has no value whatsoever in the long run. Teams often make plans in their formative stages that are never implemented once training begins. The bottom line is that *good intentions are meaningless unless they're translated into solid and committed practice.* In this regard there are a few simple rules to follow.

- Every team needs two types of meetings—Business and Communicaton.

- These meetings are an integral part of training; they are held separately and at regularly scheduled times.

- Once scheduled, meetings take priority over jumping. It's okay to change the day or time of a meeting for logistical reasons or to accommodate weather conditions, but it's not okay to eliminate a meeting (especially a Communication Meeting) in order to fit in more jumps. That sacrifices quality for quantity and ultimately undermines team integrity.

Business Meetings

As the name implies, these meetings are designed to discuss and decide logistical and business issues. Although disagreement and heated debate are bound to occur at times, this is not a forum to vent feelings and work through relationship problems with other teammates. As much as possible, the content should remain factual and concrete, while the process should involve brainstorming and the general sharing of information. Many teams designate the team captain as the leader of this meeting while others prefer a system of rotating leadership or, on occasion, no leadership at all. Depending on your needs and preferences, all three methods work. Pick one, try it, and be flexible enough to change if it's not working for you.

Communication Meetings

The Art of Sharing
Feelings and emotions are a fundamental part of team dynamics and need to be expressed in a healthy constructive manner. Otherwise, they accumulate and eventually interfere with functioning and performance. Communication Meetings are designed to allow members to share their feelings regarding team issues as well as relationships with teammates.

While there are a variety of meeting formats to accomplish this, one of the simplest and most often used is called "Pass the Rock." In it an object (a rock if you wish) is held by a team member who has something to say. While holding this object, that person has the floor to express what's on his or her mind, without interruption. When finished, the object is passed to the next person who wishes to speak. Another format is called "Round Robin." This involves going around the room in consecutive order from one person to the next, speaking one at a time, in turn. In both formats the meeting ends only when everyone has had a chance to speak.

Because these meetings are sometimes emotionally charged, it is important that everyone be in complete agreement with both the format and structure at the outset. Generally, active leadership is not necessary as the structure itself provides the control and direction. Regardless of what format you use, the golden rule is that **no one gets interrupted while sharing**. If this rule is broken, anyone can momentarily stop the meeting and remind members of their agreement to listen while others speak.

It is important to note that these meetings are not an excuse to be verbally abusive and "dump" on a teammate, although it is okay to articulate powerful emotions. The short-term goal is to communicate with fairness and authenticity in order to release pent-up feelings, resolve conflicts, and permit sharing among team members. *The long-term goal is team cohesion and the strengthening of team relationships.*

The Art of Listening

Communication is an exchange. Real listening, as compared to just hearing, requires open-mindedness, willingness, and undivided attention.   This is no small thing; in fact, it is probably the most difficult and strenuous aspect of communication.   The freedom to share—to fully express yourself and speak your mind—must be matched by a commitment on the part of the listener to be totally engaged with you in the present moment.   Otherwise, why bother opening up? Why risk being vulnerable with an audience that seems disinterested or uncaring?

When your teammates are sharing at a Communication Meeting, it doesn't matter if you're tired, angry, or don't particularly like who they are or what they're saying. At this meeting your responsibility is to rise to the occasion and listen deeply and attentively, regardless of how you may feel.   I cannot stress this enough. All members of the team need to leave this meeting knowing that they were heard by their teammates and knowing that each of their teammates respected them enough to carefully listen to what they were saying. This is a huge responsibility.

Listening must be as genuine as possible. This is not about pretending to listen; it is about being open to new ideas and discovering the value in what someone is saying, regardless of your opinion. It is about paying attention to the message, even if you do not like the messenger. It is about putting yourself in someone else's shoes in an effort to understand them, and not rejecting what they say before they've even said it. Yes, it can be extraordinarily difficult to listen with openness to someone you're annoyed with or disagree with, but when you joined the team, you accepted this responsibility. Besides, when it's your turn to share, that's exactly the kind of respect you'll want from your teammates.

Accentuate the Positives

A common oversight at Communication Meetings is the tendency to focus solely on the discharge of negative feelings and completely bypass the sharing of positive ones. This causes teams to "live in the problem and not the solution" and overlook what is working and focus exclusively on what is not. The result is often a team that is off balance and insecure.

The full expression of positive along with negative emotions is essential to build and maintain trust and fellowship. If the positives go unexpressed, a priceless opportunity to empower the team and immeasurably strengthen it is lost. While it may be important to tell your teammates how much they annoy you on occasion, it is equally important to communicate how much you appreciate them and why. It is important to be very clear in sharing what you see as their strengths—the gifts they bring to the team—and to be specific about how they've added to your growth and development or how their input has enriched your life personally. *It is essential that this positive sharing occur at a formalized team meeting and not just in casual conversation.*

I've seen some people initially recoil at the notion of saying warm, positive things out loud in front of others. They find it embarrassing and would prefer not to do it at all, or at least do it in private. But my experience has also shown that this discomfort evaporates almost immediately once the sharing begins. And the reason is obvious.

It feels good to be appreciated by your peers for your skill, hard work, and growth, and to be publicly acknowledged for your contribution to a team effort. It also feels good to express gratitude and appreciation to your teammates, and to let them know how their unique talents and abilities have made a difference for you. This is fellowship at its best and should be encouraged whenever possible. It fortifies a team from the inside out and fosters confidence and a healthy interdependence. It is one of the unique opportunities that only teamwork can provide.

Positive Sharing and Listening Exercise

This is best done at the end of a Business or Communication meeting and takes ten to fifteen minutes. After a short break and some thoughtful consideration, every member of the team decides on one or two things they appreciate, respect, or wish to acknowledge about each one of their teammates. It can be a skill or ability, a personality trait or characteristic, recognition of effort, hard work, or improvement, etc. The format for sharing this is as follows:

- "George, I appreciate how much hard work you've put into improving your flying skills lately. I've really noticed a difference and it's made the team much stronger."
- "Kathy, I have a lot of respect for your leadership abilities on this team. You're always willing to take on new responsibilities and move this team in a positive direction. You never hesitate to rise to the occasion."
- "Bill, I want to acknowledge you for the great job you've done in developing a positive working relationship with manifest. Our turn around time is much quicker these days. Without your efforts, things wouldn't run half as smoothly as they do."
- "Jill, I appreciate how you're always willing to spend time with me when I need to vent something. Thanks for being such a great listener."

There are two important rules to follow in this exercise.

1. Make your statements brief and to the point. No long winded speeches are necessary; a few sentences will do.
2. The person on the receiving end must listen only. No response is permitted. This is not a two-way conversation. This can be difficult. Most of us are not used to listening quietly when positive things are said about us. We have a tendency to reply in some way with either a comment or joke. However, listening quietly allows us to fully absorb and integrate this positive acknowledgment without diluting it with talk or laughter. It may not be easy, but practice makes perfect, and the benefits of this exercise are well worth the practice.

Success and Achievement Stories

Pick any time in your life when you successfully achieved a goal or overcame a problem or obstacle. It can be something that required advanced thought and planning such as an athletic achievement, learning to play a musical instrument, or earning a college degree, or a spontaneous situation where you suddenly had to mobilize yourself, as in overcoming an illness or coping with a personal loss. It can be as simple as having changed a negative attitude to a positive one, or how you learned to cope with someone you didn't like.

Team members can alternate telling their stories at Communication Meetings. This should be done with enthusiasm, pride, and even a sense of bragging as if you were sharing it in order to motivate others to greatness (you are).

An added benefit comes to those who are willing to write their story prior to sharing it. Writing is a powerful way to re-live an experience and reinforce its learning value. (Good writing skills are not necessary for this exercise.) If you prefer, you can simply outline your story before telling it. If you absolutely refuse to write you can share it ad lib.

Regardless of your method, your story should address the following:
- What was your goal? That is, what were you trying to accomplish?
- Why was the goal important to you?
- How did you feel before, during, and after the experience?
- What actions did you take to enable you to reach your goal?
- Were there times when you wanted to quit trying but persevered in spite of those feelings?
- What is the moral of your story? What did you learn from this experience that has helped you in other areas of your life and might be of benefit to others?

Success stories are shared for the following reasons:
- They keep you plugged in to positive action and change.
- They help you know your teammates better.
- They allow you to benefit from the creative problem solving techniques used by others.
- Strength and courage are contagious. When you're exposed to those qualities in others, the same are generated in you.

Some Additional Suggestions

- **Learn to be comfortable with being uncomfortable.**
  When things don't go your way, allow yourself to
  experience the disappointment without overreacting to the
  situation or suppressing your feelings. Be aware of your
  discomfort and how it impacts your thinking and
  physiology. Notice what part of your body feels tense, and
  listen carefully to the dialogue you're having in your head.
  At least for a few moments, don't judge anything and don't
  change anything. Just observe your reactions.

- **Practice your listening skills anywhere/anytime you can.**
  Whenever you can, at home, at work, or on the drop zone,
  make yourself sit quietly and _listen_ to what someone is
  saying. Resist the urge to interrupt or jump in with your
  opinion. Temporarily see life from the other person's
  perspective and try to fully understand their point of view.
  Take a good look at yourself through their eyes and notice
  what you see. How receptive do you appear to be? Do you
  look like someone who's really listening or someone who's
  "shut down" and just waiting for a pause in the conversation
  so you can jump in with your opinion? Given an option,
  would you want to have this conversation with you?

- **You don't have to attend every argument you're invited
  to.** Instead, play the "It's All My Fault Game." Make a
  decision that the next time you get into an argument you're
  going to pretend that you're the one who's wrong. Then
  silently ask yourself, "What can I do to resolve this
  conflict?" This takes an enormous amount of resolve and
  internal strength to accomplish. When we argue, most of us
  get very attached to the notion of being "right" and
  forcefully resist giving up any ground. Such an attitude on
  our part tends to increase resistance in our adversary, limit

our own awareness, and prevent us from finding solutions to the problem. Both sides are preoccupied with proving their "rightness," and genuine listening grinds to a halt. The result is a lose/lose situation. It is only when someone becomes willing to "soften" their position that the possibility of a win/win situation is created. The choice is up to you.

- **Practice being vulnerable and let others help.** Allow your teammates to see some of your weaknesses. Put your pride and ego aside, welcome constructive criticism, and give others the opportunity to help you improve at something. It's a good feeling when someone asks us for help. We feel trusted and appreciated. Let your teammates have that good feeling. I promise they'll give it back.

- **Extend yourself to someone who annoys you.**   You don't have to become best friends—just allow yourself to get a little bit closer and notice what you see. Often we get annoyed with people because we see in them what we don't like in ourselves. They become unpleasant reminders of what we're trying to avoid. Other times we get annoyed because we're convinced that our way of doing something is the best and only way to do it. It becomes inconceivable that someone else might have an equally good idea. Sometimes we get annoyed because we're just plain grouchy, impatient, or defiant in that moment and we're not about to give anybody any slack. Whatever the case, tolerating and accepting what you dislike can only strengthen you mentally and emotionally. So if for no other reason, do it for that one.

- **Only complain to someone who can do something about your complaint.**   The next time you catch yourself complaining—Stop—and then ask yourself if the person you're complaining to can really help resolve your problem.

If not, then stop complaining immediately because you're just wasting your time and energy. In fact, you're actually keeping yourself stuck in the problem by playing victim. Instead, see a big red STOP sign in your mind and either end the conversation completely or change it to something productive.

It's okay to share a problem with someone and brainstorm about possible solutions, but complaining is a dead end. (And we all know the difference.)

- **Resist the urge to gossip.** Actually, gossip is a form of complaining. It's *me* telling *you* something unfavorable about *them* that's none of my business to begin with. It's a two-way interaction that requires both participants. Even if all I'm doing is listening to someone gossip or complain, I'm cooperating fully, because without me there would be no conversation.

  Complaining and gossiping are deadly viruses that ultimately destroy what teams work so hard to build. The results are disastrous. Before long, problems get sidestepped instead of resolved and cliques begin to form within teams. People start whispering and talking behind closed doors about issues that should be addressed openly at team meetings. Members start planning covert strategies and "ganging up" on one another.

  Avoid this behavior at all cost. If you see it happening on your team, encourage that person to share his or her feelings at a Communications Meeting. None of us is perfect and most of us have a tendency to gossip and complain. But if we agree as a team to monitor each other and ourselves in this regard, then we have the opportunity to eliminate these problems before they eliminate our team.

CHAPTER 8

Video Games

~The Creative Use of Visualization and Imagery~

Life is on the wire. The rest is just waiting.
Carl Wallenda

Let's begin by distinguishing between visualization and imagery. Strictly speaking, visualization is the creation of a *visual* representation of an object or experience in your mind. It refers to *seeing* something in your imagination as if you were viewing it on a screen. To visualize a skydive for instance is to watch it happen in your mind.

Imagery, on the other hand, is much more dynamic and comprehensive because it utilizes all of your senses to create an experience that closely approximates reality. Instead of just *seeing* the skydive happen, in imagery you might also *hear* the plane's engine, *smell* the jet fuel, *feel* the wind on your body and the grips in your hands, maybe even *taste* the dryness in your mouth or the flavor of the chewing gum or cigarette you just discarded. In imagery, you control all of the variables.

Even though your conscious mind knows the difference between what's real and imagined, as far as your body and unconscious mind are concerned, a carefully designed and executed imagery is identical to experiencing reality. In fact, the physiological and emotional effects are indistinguishable from those that would occur if the event were actually happening. Consequently, the potential for learning and insight is enormous.

There are, however, two conditions that block our effective use of both visualization and imagery. The first involves our limited belief in their training value. Although most of us would agree that these tools enhance learning to some extent, the majority of us are not aware of the immense impact they can have on our performance, positively or negatively, regardless of our skill level. As a result, we utilize these mental tools much less than we should. We tend to visualize briefly on the ground prior to a jump and again in the plane on the way to altitude. We may even add a kinesthetic component (taking grips) to the visualization but that's pretty much the extent of it for most skydivers.

The second condition blocking our use of visualization and imagery is our lack of knowledge on the subject. Through no fault of our own, we simply don't know how to use these tools correctly because we've never been taught. We certainly don't learn these techniques in any formal educational setting, and most sport psychology or peak performance books barely touch on the subject. They go so far as to prescribe the use of visualization and imagery, but don't tell us exactly how to do it. Rarely explained are the different training results that can be achieved by manipulating what are called the **submodalities** of a visualization: the size of a mental picture, color, contrast, brightness, texture, angle, focus, speed, direction, perspective, foreground, background, etc.

In his book, *Using Your Brain For A Change*, Richard Bandler, co-founder of Neuro-Linguistic Programming (NLP), lists over seventy possible submodalities that can be altered to achieve different effects. It probably never dawned on most of us that we could increase the power of a visualization and consequently its learning benefit by adding or erasing one part of a mental picture and leaving the rest intact, or bringing a picture closer (making it larger) or moving it farther away (making it smaller), or changing a moving picture to a snapshot or vice-versa.   Other possibilities are slow-motion or freeze-frame or reverse action or associated viewing (being in the picture), or dissociated viewing (watching the picture)... the combinations are endless.

So how does altering these submodalities enhance the effects of mental training on skydiving performance?   It's simple.   Every correct repetition of a skill strengthens the performance blueprint of that skill.   The more powerful the visualization and imagery, the greater the learning and the deeper you groove that blueprint.   You can't control all of the variables in an actual skydive, but you can in your imagination with practice.

Many of the "greats" have been systematically applying these creative techniques for years and seem to know intuitively how and why to use these tools. The groundbreaking science of Neuro-Linguistic Programming has been exploring this area since 1977.   The results are startling and incredible!

Whether you're a world-class competitor or a weekend fun jumper, there's no end to what you can do once you begin playing with some of these tools.   Your only limit is the extent of your imagination and the degree of your willingness to experiment.   What I'm offering here is a starting point—a place to begin.   Then, who knows?

Start Where You Are

We all have amazing imaginations.   Some people, myself included, have difficulty visualizing clear, vivid pictures but do just fine with imagery.   If you ask me to close my eyes and visualize an apple, the best I can generally do is create something small and round that I identify as an apple.   I tend to see little detail and can't differentiate it from a ball or any other round object for that matter. However, I can taste it, feel it, and hear it crunch when I take an imaginary bite out of it.

The visual modality is clearly not my dominant way of imagining. I share this because I've met many people over the years who have similar difficulty visualizing clearly and worry that their mental abilities must be defective if they can't see vivid pictures in their minds like others can.

If you fall into this category, please don't think of yourself as having a problem. You simply experience your imagination differently. In fact, thinking that you're broken only causes you to work harder to visualize, and all that does is jam up the works even more. The fact that someone can see clear and vivid pictures in his mind either indicates that his primary sense modality is visual, or he's had the opportunity to practice this skill frequently over the years.

Your primary sense modality may be auditory or kinesthetic or olfactory. Actually, all of us turn out to have slightly different combinations to varying degrees. My friend Ellen, for instance, is capable of visualizing an apple in detail to the point of seeing shades of color, exact ripeness, imperfections the apple might have, etc. She's an artist who's developed this ability over time. While her visual acuity is high, it doesn't necessarily predispose her to being a better athlete. Someone with a highly developed kinesthetic or auditory sense is just as capable.

Imagery

The use of imagery tends to be more effective in emotional learning (confidence, self-esteem, etc.) and the development of muscle memory, because in imagery you actually experience yourself in the activity you're imagining. On a very real level your mind and body are participating in the event. It's like watching an exciting movie in the theater; during a chase scene your body reacts as if you were actually in the chase. Your heart rate, skin temperature, blood pressure, body chemistry, and emotions all fluctuate. Learning occurs on a conscious and unconscious level whether you're aware of it or not. Generally speaking, the more senses you engage in imagery the greater the learning or training effect, although this varies individually.

Visualization

The use of visualization tends to assist more with cognitive learning such as remembering, creating, designing, engineering, etc. It allows us to view and evaluate from a more distant and detached perspective. Seeing the larger picture enables us to make adjustments in form or technique and gives us the opportunity to be more objective in assessing the overall situation.

Visualization is often the first mental tool we use when learning a new skill. We can repeatedly visualize the perfect execution of a move in our mind to imprint it in our memory. Then we can use imagery to increase our mastery of the other dynamics involved in that particular moment of performance.

What I'm providing here is a generalized framework with some definitions. Consider that the real power in training is unique for each individual and arises naturally when we allow ourselves to play. So by all means approach the following exercises in that spirit. Don't worry about a "right" or "wrong" way of doing it. The best results appear when we're curious and relaxed—when we engage an image with the intensity and fascination of a child. In those special moments, these games can sometimes provide more learning for improving form, cognition, and muscle memory than an actual skydive.

It's true, although I'm not suggesting substituting one for the other. Nothing can replace a real skydive, and nothing should. But used together they reinforce one another and open up an incredible realm of possibility for heightened learning. They make one hell of a team.

> If you want to improve your imagery and visualization skills you can learn to do so through certain types of exercises that are beyond the scope of this book.   Some excellent resources are *Visioning* by Lucia Capacchione, and *The Power of Visualization* (an audio cassette series) by Lee Pulos. Additional resources are available through Nightingale-Conant Corporation, 1-800-525-9000 or www.nightingale.com.

Practice Makes Perfect

These games work if you work them. If you want the maximum benefit from mental training, you have to train mentally every chance you get. All of the technology in the world won't replace the learning that comes from repetition. In that respect there are no short cuts to peak performance.   Latch on to exercises that you enjoy and that work for you, and practice them repeatedly and consistently throughout the week. Practice week after week, month after month; the importance of your goal should be the only determining factor in how much time and energy you invest. Enjoy the process; it really can be fun. In fact, the more you enjoy it, the more you'll learn.

Let The Games Begin

These exercises are meant to be fully experienced and not just read. Take your time and move through them very slowly.

Prior to beginning most of them it's important to clear your mind of any distractions. One way to do this is by sitting quietly and breathing normally with your eyes closed for a few minutes. The goal is to be relaxed, not sleepy. Imagine that any stress or tension you have is draining out of your body and either into the ground or into the air around you. You're ready to begin an exercise once you feel calm and centered.

Game One: THE DIRECTOR

Goal:
- To experience the effects of altering the submodalities of a visualization.

Time Element:
- 5 to 10 minutes

How to Play:
- Picture an enjoyable experience in your mind. It can be anything you like, skydiving or not. Now begin by making the picture in your mind a little brighter and see what effect that has on your emotions. Take your time and don't rush this. Now slowly increase the brightness level and notice what happens. Now increase it to the max.
- Next, repeat the above procedure only this time make the picture darker. Generally, a brighter picture will enhance a feeling of enjoyment, although a picture that's too bright might have the opposite effect.   Making an enjoyable picture darker tends to diminish the positive feelings. Conversely, making an unhappy picture darker tends to diminish the negative feelings. (This is a good thing to know.)
- Using the above method, now make the original picture larger and experience the difference it makes. Then make it smaller and notice what happens. As with brightness, generally a larger picture will intensify a feeling and a smaller picture will diminish it.
- Continue experimenting with some of the different submodalities that I mentioned earlier, such as sound, color, contrast, angle, speed, freeze frame, etc. and notice the impact these changes have on you. What you'll see after a little bit of practice is how easy it becomes to modify your

feelings and emotions simply by altering the characteristics of the picture you're seeing in your mind.

Afterthoughts and Reflections:

- Remember that your reactions are unique to you. There are no right or wrong responses to altering submodalities. If brightness decreases a feeling for you but increases one for your friend, then so be it. The goal is to learn how mental pictures work for you, so you can design them to enhance your own learning.

  For instance, if you just made a crummy skydive and can't shake the negative feelings, picture that jump in your mind (as if it ever really left), and start changing the submodalities. If you've been practicing this exercise on a regular basis you'll be able to dilute its negative impact fairly quickly and move on. You can always go back to it later for learning purposes if you want to. Or, if you just made a jump that was moderately successful, you can make some changes in the picture to highlight the positives and minimize the rest. (Wouldn't that be a nicer feeling to carry with you on the next jump?)

  If this sounds just a little too good to be true, please be assured that it's not. Even a minimum of practice and effort in this area will yield impressive results. All too often we tend to automatically and unconsciously change submodalities in a negative fashion without even realizing what we're doing. We make a "mountain out of a molehill" or we see a "dark or dim future" or we "blow something out of proportion."

  What I'm suggesting is that we can make a molehill out of a mountain any time we want to. We can change a dark future to a bright one if we so desire. And why not blow some positive stuff out of proportion for a change! Give it a try.

Game Two: THE MOVIE

Goal:
- To improve cognitive learning and muscle memory.
- To develop new skills and strengthen existing ones.

Time Element:
- 5 to 10 minutes

How to Play:
- Part 1 - Visualize a skydive that you would like to learn. Begin by seeing your performance as if you are watching it on video. Run it through as many times as you like until you know it well. If it's a complicated dive you might want to break it down into sections and view one at a time.
- Part 2 - Repeat the above procedure only this time use imagery to fully experience yourself being in the skydive as compared to just watching it. Engage as many of your senses as possible. Your goal is to end the exercise feeling as if you've just made a skydive.

Afterthoughts and Reflections:
- An effective variation for RW is to do the above procedure while lying on a creeper or on the floor at home. CRW can do it standing up with their hands holding imaginary toggles. Sit flyers can sit in a chair. The idea is to attempt to approximate your body position as closely as you can. Golfers and tennis players often do these exercises standing in a set position with their club or racquet in hand. Basketball players often visualize while standing at an imaginary foul line. Archers mime every movement of shooting an arrow with no equipment in their hands. This kind of practice amplifies imagery detail skill and reinforces the body's belief that the activity is really occurring.

Game Three: I'M A CHAMPION

Goal:
- Confidence building and identity modification.

Time Element:
- 5 to 10 minutes or more

How to Play:
- Watch a world-class skydiving performance on video. Pick one of the skydivers and pretend that it's you. Really get into the fantasy. See yourself on the screen performing with incredible ease and ability. Notice how your moves feel natural and effortless. You are a champion. You know how it feels to execute a perfect skydive. Watch it over and over and over.

Afterthoughts and Reflections:
- Some people hesitate to play this game of pretending because it sounds like something a child would do. And that's precisely what it is.   Children often immerse themselves so deeply in fantasy that they temporarily forget who they are and what they're capable of. This allows them to be capable of so much more. And that's exactly why I'm suggesting you do it.
- On one hand, our identity keeps us safe and secure in the world, but on the other, it limits us to a set of self-imposed boundaries and parameters. We get used to and comfortable with perceiving ourselves in a fixed way—often we become stagnant. This game provides an opportunity to forget your identity temporarily and assume someone else's. You can have yours back whenever you want it. And when you do, you'll bring some positive aspects of your assumed identity with you. You will develop a better sense of certain skills that may have eluded you before and increased your

confidence in your ability to perform.

Even if you're already a world-class performer you can assume the attributes of someone who's further along than you are in certain areas. The idea is to model someone with skills and abilities superior to your own. So for five minutes a day, allow yourself to be the best in the world. If you're already the best, then set you sights even higher. "Fake it 'til you make it." See and feel yourself executing moves flawlessly and effortlessly in your mind and you will see improvement, not only in your confidence, but in your technical abilities as well. I guarantee it.

Game Four: BACK AND FORTH

Goal:
- To perfect a movement or sequence.

Time Element:
- 5 to 10 minutes

How to Play:
- Pick a movement or transition in a skydive that you're having difficulty mastering.
- Using visualization, mentally practice it a few times in forward slow motion and then once or twice in reverse slow motion.   Now picture the perfect execution of this movement at normal speed. Take a moment to enjoy the results. Visualize this perfect version at least two more times.
- Now do the exact same exercise using imagery instead of visualization.
- Now go and do the skydive for real.

Game Five: FOCUS—DISTRACT—FOCUS

Goal:
- Improve focus, concentration, and distraction control.

Time Element:
- 2 to 5 minutes

How to Play:
- Begin visualizing a particular skydive and deliberately distract yourself by thinking of something else. Immediately refocus as quickly as you can. Practice by repeatedly distracting yourself until you're able to regain focus quickly and easily. Keep this a game and don't do it to the point of frustration. If you find yourself getting annoyed, do something else.

Afterthoughts and Reflections:
- A useful variation is to have someone else provide the distraction at random intervals during your visualization. They can even be creative with their method of distracting you. This can be a great team exercise with members alternating as distracters. Better yet, ask your video person to do the honors.

Game Six: FOCUSED BREATHING

Goal:
- To develop and maintain relaxed attention while learning to gently and efficiently refocus.

Time Element:
- 5 to 20 minutes

How to Play:
- Practice breathing awareness for ten minutes a day (or longer if you like.) Find a relaxed position where you won't fall asleep. Sitting upright in a comfortable chair works well. Leave your arms and legs uncrossed to allow for unrestricted blood circulation. Simply focus on your breathing at one of two points: either the tip of your nose where the air enters and exits, or your abdomen as it rises and falls.
- There is nothing else to do. When thoughts enter your mind just notice them, let them pass, and refocus on your breathing. Although you might become distracted with countless thoughts during a five or ten minute period, the point is to be able to notice the distraction and then gently and simply return your focus to your breath.

Afterthoughts and Reflections:
- Be flexible with this. If you find it easy, aim for fifteen to twenty minute periods. If you find it difficult, begin with five-minute sessions and work your way up. A variation is to mentally say "in" as you inhale and "out" as you exhale while keeping the focus at the tip of the nose or the abdomen. The goal is to cultivate "relaxed attention," which is a necessary element of peak performance.

Game Seven: MANTRA

Goal:

- To strengthen and internalize a particular area of learning.

Time Required:
- None

How to Play:

- Prior to a skydive, repeat a word to yourself out loud or in a whisper, that signifies your mental goal for this jump. For example: Repeat the word "calm," or "relax," or "focus," or "arch." Start doing this ten to twenty minutes prior to the skydive and after a few minutes repeat the word internally instead of aloud, unless you prefer to keep repeating it aloud. Within a short time the word will begin reverberating in your mind, and like a mantra, will keep repeating itself long after you've consciously stopped saying it. With practice you'll find that you can be holding a conversation with someone and still hear the word echoing inside of you.

Afterthoughts and Reflections:

- What makes this effective is that your training goal becomes internalized and allows training to occur simultaneously on both a conscious and unconscious level. Eventually, you're not even consciously aware of an internal focus, but you have one nonetheless.

Game Eight: SMILE

Goal:
- Instantaneous stress reduction.

Time Element:
- One second, maybe two

How to Play:
- SMILE. When you feel stressed or tense or angry or upset, just smile. Make yourself smile and hold it for as long as you can, even if you have to force it. If you find yourself wanting to laugh, do it.

Afterthoughts and Reflections:
- The simple act of smiling instantly reduces stress, anxiety, and tension. The pleasant feelings associated with a smile are so deeply imprinted in our muscle memory, that our emotional state automatically and involuntarily changes as the muscles in our face form that particular shape. Stress and tension are instantly reduced and often eliminated completely.

    Please try this one. Smile now if you like. Come on, just for a second. Nobody's watching. It's simple, easy to do, and best of all it's very effective. And it's available anytime, anywhere, under any circumstances. It's also contagious and can do wonders for those around you.
- It's especially useful as you set-up in the door of the plane. In fact the combination of breathing and smiling together can do wonders for an exit.

Game Nine: SECURE THE ANCHOR

Goal:
- Distraction control, arousal management, stress reduction.

Time Element:
- 5 to 10 minutes

How to Play:
- Using imagery, experience a past skydive that was particularly satisfying and memorable—one that left you feeling confident and empowered. As you create this vivid picture, allow the positive feelings associated with it to fully develop in your mind and body. At the height of these feelings, take your thumb, index finger and middle finger of either hand and pinch them together. Hold it for about ten seconds as you experience these powerful and positive emotions, then release them.
- This is called anchoring—the process of linking an action to an emotion or feeling. Each time you repeat this process you reinforce the connection. Before long, you'll be able to pinch those fingers together and create a positive feeling without having to do the imagery. The response will be virtually automatic. You can use this technique to empower yourself, control your arousal level, reduce stress or tension, or create an overall feeling of well-being.

Afterthoughts and Reflections:
- Every day we create new anchors and experience the effects of old ones. Billions of dollars are spent each year in advertising to entice us to buy products by anchoring (connecting) them to songs, slogans, colors, logos, values (e.g. masculine, feminine, thin, muscular, wealthy. . .) etc. How many times have you heard a song on the radio that immediately anchored you to a powerful feeling about a

relationship or situation?

- There's a variation of this game called "stacking the anchors." It's played by imagining a succession of different positive experiences and pinching your fingers together at the height of each experience. They can all be from the same area, such as four or five skydiving experiences, or you can access powerful events from other areas in your life such as family, friends, work, etc.

- A second variation is to anchor a feeling to a particular word instead of an action. Rather than pinching your fingers, you might focus on repeating a special word while you're imaging. This connects a positive feeling to that word. Some athletes use words that are already powerful anchors in their lives. Many use the names of loved ones, past or present. Some use the various names of God to empower them. The choice is up to you. Whether it's an action or a word, the results will be the same if you've taken time to develop the anchor properly.

Game Ten: TOTAL RECALL

Goal:
- Awareness or mindfulness training.

Time Element:
- 5 minutes before and after a skydive

How to Play:
- Visualize an upcoming skydive as you normally would and then repeat the visualization in slow motion once or twice noticing each detail of the dive.
- Then actually go and do the skydive, with video.
- Before watching the video, recall as much of the skydive as you can by visualizing it once again at normal speed and then again in slow motion. Write this down if you can.
- Now watch the video and compare the accuracy of your recall.

Afterthoughts and Reflections:
- The nature of skydiving is such that sensory and emotional overload often interfere with and limit our awareness. The pressure of competition can have the same effect. Utilizing visual slow motion can enable us to see detail that might normally go unnoticed. If you're particularly good at visualization, you might want to experiment with freeze-framing parts of your dive for closer inspection.

Game Eleven: JUST IMAGINE

Goal:
- Create your future.
- Become familiar with success.

Time Element:
- 5 to 10 minutes

How to Play:
- Take a moment to relax and get centered. Choose any one of your goals. It can be a small one or your life's dream. Using rich sensory detail begin imagining the achievement of this goal. Make this internal experience as real and joyful as possible. Notice what you see, hear, feel, smell and taste in the state of *having accomplished your goal.* Allow yourself to fully embrace the feelings of joy and satisfaction that accompany this attainment. How are others reacting to you? What are they saying? What are you saying and thinking to yourself? What does your body feel like? Create this scenario as if you are a great movie director. Spare no detail. And keep it positive.
- Play it over until you've created an Academy Award winning movie.
- Run it as often as possible.

Afterthoughts and Reflections:
- For most of us, our inability to achieve something has very little to do with whether or not we're capable of achieving it. It's about whether we believe we're capable of achieving it, whether we believe we deserve to achieve it, and whether we can truly see ourselves achieving it.
- More often than not our thinking reflects the accepted notion of "I'll believe it when I see it," when the truth is usually the opposite—"I'll see it when I believe it." We

tend to be cynical and analytical, always requiring concrete proof of something's existence before we'll accept it as reality. Paradoxically, most goals are achieved after first creating and imagining them in our mind. As the goal becomes an internal reality, the leap required to attain it diminishes.

- Imagery provides the opportunity to design and simulate the experience we desire. On both conscious and unconscious levels it allows us to anticipate the event happening so that when it does, it comes as no surprise to us. In a sense, we've been preparing for it and expecting it all along.

CHAPTER 9

Meditation

~The Difference It Can Make~

*Enlightenment is an accident
But some activities make you accident prone.*
Zen Master

Twenty years ago if you saw an athlete sitting cross-legged on a cushion burning incense and chanting a mantra, you'd probably question their mental health or at least think they were weird or "far out" as they used to say. But if you claim to be an athlete today and don't practice meditation in some form, you're missing out on one of the most powerful training tools available. The jury is in; the verdict is clear. There are now scores of scientific studies that conclusively prove the immeasurable benefits of meditation, and there are thousands of world-class athletes who meditate regularly as part of their training regimen in order to achieve the following results:

- A decreased need for oxygen and a subsequent decrease in breathing rate.
- The development of a more stable and efficient blood chemistry.

- An increased ability to respond both physically and emotionally to stressful situations.
- Heightened awareness and distraction control.
- A reduction in the formation of lactic acid and a decrease in skin resistance, which are both products of stress.
- An improved balance and coherence between the right and left hemispheres and front and rear portions of the brain.
- An increased ability to learn, reflected in faster learning and greater amounts of information absorbed.
- A strengthening of the body's immune system.

And the list goes on, depending on which studies you read and which authorities you quote. Any one of the above advantages is well worth having, but the possibility of deriving all these benefits from one form of training is priceless. If results like these could be obtained in a pill, skydivers would line up around the block to get a supply and wouldn't hesitate to pay the asking price. But when the price is meditation, unfortunately, lots of us turn the other way.

It's sad to think how many readers will skip over this chapter convinced that meditation is not for them. They may have heard about it, read about it, know people who do it, and even tried it once or twice in the past. They may even be aware of some of the benefits, but still can't imagine themselves doing it. If you're one of these people—and I used to be—all I ask is that you keep reading with an open mind and consider the possibility that meditation is not what you think—that it might be for you—that it might be easy to do—and that it might even be an enjoyable activity. If at the end of this chapter you still have no interest in meditation, then you've lost nothing but a few minutes of your time.

I first tried meditation about fifteen years ago. I had heard lots of interesting things about it, most of them grandiose, and was hoping it would give me some kind of a "high" or profound experience. One day I waited until I was alone in my house, disconnected the phone and turned off the television, and sat quietly in a chair in my living room. I told myself that for the next fifteen minutes I was going to sit still and not think of anything. I was going to meditate.

I sat quietly and waited for what seemed like an eternity, but nothing extraordinary happened. In fact, it was pure torture. It was so boring I thought I was going to go crazy. Making myself sit still with absolutely nothing to do was bad enough, but forcing myself not to think of anything was sheer madness. The more I tried not to think, the more thoughts I had. A thought would come, I'd chase it away, and ten more would come to replace it. It was a raging battle. Stressed and exhausted I quit after about ten minutes. This stuff was not for me. Meditation was for spiritual people, or Buddhists or intellectuals maybe—but definitely not for me.

What I can see now is how little I knew about meditation at that time. In my zeal I was simply copying something I had seen, without having any understanding of what it was all about or how to proceed. And my expectations were totally unrealistic in that I was expecting some deep metaphysical experience to occur. It never did.

Ten years later I tried it again after reading an article that clearly explained the process and highlighted some of the practical benefits. I really wanted and needed those benefits, so I was willing to give it another try. Only this time I was approaching it differently.

- I decided to sit quietly for only five minutes instead of fifteen. (I knew I could endure anything for only five minutes.)
- I gave myself permission to move and adjust my body position if I felt uncomfortable.
- Instead of trying to stop all my thoughts (which I now know is impossible) I simply focused my attention on my breathing and allowed the thoughts to come and go.

- I reminded myself not to expect anything extraordinary. Benefits would be subtle and come over time.

In those next five minutes a thousand thoughts came and went and I got distracted more times than I can remember. But each time I did, I gently returned my attention to my breathing. When it was over, nothing monumental had occurred. It wasn't a great experience, but it wasn't a bad one either. The good news was that I had survived. I had meditated. I had finally done it. What next? Meditate again. So I made a personal commitment to meditate on a trial basis for five minutes a day, three days a week for a month, and then evaluate whether I wanted to continue. I was determined to give this thing a fair chance before I dismissed it again.

A couple of weeks into it, I found myself looking forward to this quiet time. I was really beginning to enjoy the relaxed feeling I got both during and afterwards. At one point, when my work schedule got hectic and I missed a few days, I was surprised to find myself eager to return to it. I increased the time to ten minutes, then twenty. I began setting my alarm a half-hour earlier in the morning to start my day with meditation, and I've been doing it ever since.

It's still nothing magical and I've had no revelations or deep spiritual experiences as a result of it. But over time I have noticed that I'm able to relax more deeply, take more things in stride, and not get as stressed as I used to over certain situations. And three years later it dawned on me that I hadn't even had a cold since I began meditating.

Is it a coincidence? Has this stuff really strengthened my immune system? I honestly don't know. But I do know that I used to get sick at least once, sometimes twice, a year. Now I have more energy, a longer attention span, and am able to focus and concentrate with less effort. But even without these benefits, I have grown to like meditation—to really enjoy this special time with myself. It has become a great way to begin each day.

So I invite you to try it for a short period of time to see if it makes a difference in your life and in your skydiving. The best way to begin is to pick a set time each day when you won't be disturbed. Find a quiet place, preferably in your home, or if that's not possible you can meditate sitting in your car if you need to. Having a timer helps so you don't spend your meditation wondering when the time is up or if you've meditated long enough. It also adds an element of consistency to your practice. Your eyes can be opened or closed although most people prefer to close their eyes in the beginning. If you choose to keep them open it's best to focus at a spot on the floor at about a forty-five degree angle. Don't stare at the spot but allow your eyes to gently gaze at it. Decide how long you wish to meditate and set the timer accordingly. Then focus your attention on your breathing in one of two places—either at the tip of your nose where the air enters and exits, or at your diaphragm or stomach where it rises and falls. You can sit in a chair or lie on your back as long as you don't have the tendency to fall asleep on your back. The point is to be comfortable but also alert. Meditation is not about going to sleep; on the contrary, it's about full and total awareness.

One of the first things you become aware of in meditation is all of the thoughts swimming around in your head. As you begin to get quiet they start flooding into your mind. Thoughts like, "Why am I doing this?" "When is it going to be over?" "Meditation doesn't work anyway." "I have more important things to do." "This is probably going to be a waste of my time." "I need to fix my car." "I have to call Mary back." "When are the Nationals this year?" etc.

The point in meditation is to simply notice the distracting thoughts you're having and return your attention to your breath each time. Sometimes you'll get absorbed in a thought before you even realize you've been distracted. There may be a tendency to fight the thoughts and force them out of your mind, but that only makes them stronger. What you resist, persists. So be gentle with yourself in meditation. Don't fight anything. This can't be done perfectly. It's just a mental practice—a training exercise—nothing to take too seriously.

There's a saying, "Angels can fly because they take themselves lightly." By all means do this lightly and you'll discover the benefits are even greater. You'll begin to develop a neutrality or equanimity around positive and negative thoughts, and you'll notice them pass as quickly as they come.

It's like looking at a fixed point in the sky and watching the clouds as they pass by that point. You don't see where they came from and you don't follow where they're going. You don't get attached to them one way or another. You simply notice them as they pass in front of your awareness, and you let them move on. That (in a nutshell) is meditation—being in the moment with "what is."

Keep in mind, there are countless ways to meditate if the above method doesn't suit you, and there are numerous books to learn from. You can even meditate by taking a long slow walk while being mindful of your breath, sensations in your body, the elements around you, the motion of your legs and feet as you take each step, etc. For others, meditation involves sitting quietly and listening to the sounds of nature. The method you use will vary with your personal taste and the result you desire. If your purpose is to get centered and relaxed, any number of techniques will do.

In my work with skydivers and other competitive athletes, I've found that the regular practice of meditation improves the ability to control negative thinking, eliminate distraction, and regulate arousal levels.

- Over time you learn to become less attached to thoughts and the feelings they produce.
- You learn that a thought is only as powerful as the meaning you attach to it.
- You develop the ability to shift away from any thought, positive or negative, by focusing on your breath.

- You begin to be selective about which thoughts you choose to pay attention to and which you choose to ignore.
- You strengthen your ability to discard unproductive negative thinking in favor of empowered thinking.
- You learn to direct your thoughts rather than have them direct you.

Imagine for a moment the value of this discipline on the ride to altitude during a competition, when you're tense or feeling distracted. You have a choice. You can fight those uncomfortable feelings or focus your attention on your breath. Your training in meditation reminds you that you can easily shift your attention. You've done it hundreds, if not thousands of times before. You're confident that you can remain positive. You've become an expert at staying focused in the present moment. The jump you're about to make is full of possibility— a tapestry about to unfold. It has nothing to do with the past. It only lives now, in the present.

Breathe.

CHAPTER 10

Performance Anxiety

The mark of a person who is in control of consciousness is the ability to focus attention at will, to be oblivious to distractions, to concentrate for as long as it takes to achieve a goal, and not longer. And the person who can do this usually enjoys the normal course of everyday life.
Mihaly Csikszentmihalyi

You've done everything right up to now: a good solid dirt dive, time on the creepers, visualization on the ground and in the plane, you're having fun, feeling strong, and have total confidence in your teammates... and suddenly WHAM! That ohmygod feeling: racing heart, sweaty palms, tight queasy stomach, fear, lots of fear. You frantically run through the dive once more in your mind testing yourself to see if you forgot anything. You think you remember it all but something doesn't feel right. Fear increases. Doubt fills your mind. It's like somebody pressed the panic button. A voice in your head screams, "If you brain lock on this one you'll ruin it for everybody. Whatever you do, don't screw up—not this time."

Not a pretty picture. Some people can't sleep because of it, some wake up with it, others get it two minutes before exit, some feel it on climb out, and some lucky ones never seem to get it at all. Of those who do, some get it bad, others just a little. What is this demon and how can we kill it?

Performance anxiety can turn brave adults into cowering children, and stellar performances into virtual disasters in the blink of an eye. We've all seen it happen and most of us have experienced it at one time or another. But contrary to what we might think, it's not a demon that comes out of nowhere. In fact, it's one we've created in the hope of killing an even larger monster.

Believe it or not, performance anxiety is a remarkable personal achievement. It's a delicately crafted and extremely powerful psychological response designed to protect us from making mistakes. In a sense, it's psychological insurance against failure. It's a behavior we've developed over time through constant experimentation. When it strikes, the brain is merely doing its job and following orders—our orders—and it's doing it very effectively.

Performance anxiety is the fusing together of two core beliefs. The first is, "mistakes are dangerous," and the second is, "worry eliminates mistakes." It's that simple. Get rid of either belief and you kill the monster. They're like nitrogen and glycerin. Taken alone each belief is relatively harmless and even contains a fragment of truth, but blended together they are explosive and deadly. Let's look at them one at a time.

"Mistakes are dangerous." Depending on the individual, danger appears in a variety of forms. Some are humiliation, embarrassment, rejection, self-condemnation, damage to self-esteem, self-image, or prestige, etc., not to mention physical danger. The belief systems supporting these fears probably originate in early childhood and by adulthood become generalized and embedded in the unconscious through constant repetition.

"Worry eliminates mistakes." In order to combat these fears and keep them at bay the psyche has developed a very powerful defense mechanism called "Worry." Someone in the grip of

performance anxiety is convinced that worry is the only way to avoid making a mistake. An inner voice demands, "If you worry enough nothing will surprise you and you won't make any mistakes. You'll be on top of the situation and ready for the unexpected."

People who suffer chronically from performance anxiety tend to be "worriers" who worry about anything and everything. They live with a constant nagging feeling that something is always about to go wrong. They frequently project negative consequences and often visualize (without realizing it most of the time) the worst possible scenario in every situation. For them, worrying has become a way of being and a natural thing to do. It's sort of an psychological "Tylenol with codeine" used to eliminate fear of any kind. The unconscious mantra is, "If in doubt, worry." Over time it's become an automatic behavior that spontaneously activates with the slightest fear or threat. Eventually it begins appearing at the most inopportune times, when it's least expected, and when it won't accomplish anything.

The paradox is that worriers use worry so they won't have to worry. On an unconscious level they are continually reminding themselves to worry in the hope that it will magically improve their performance and save them from the painful results of a mistake. Ironically however this worry magnifies any potential problems and in doing so creates the very panic and feared outcome that the worry is supposed to prevent.

The Cure

It's easy to tell you to stop worrying because most mistakes aren't really dangerous and probably won't happen to begin with. But when the panic sets in and your heart starts pounding and your palms get sweaty and you're pleading with God to help you pull this one off, how do you make this fear go away?

First of all, if you know you're prone to performance anxiety, the time to begin working on this problem is prior to making the jump, prior to boarding the plane, and even prior to coming to the drop zone. The solution needs to begin at home, at work, in your car, or anywhere else in your life you can practice being calm, centered, focused, relaxed and worry free. But we'll get back to this point in a moment.

For now, you're in the plane and you're full of fear. What can you do?

Distraction Techniques. These are some methods to shift your thinking from negative to neutral or negative to positive.

- Take a deep breath, smile (force yourself if you have to), and think about something else—anything else will do temporarily.
- Carefully examine the shapes and colors of the rig in front of you.
- Recall a scene from your funniest movie. If you have time, tell someone in the plane about it.
- Do a gear check, adjust your booties, tighten a helmet strap.
- Talk to the person next to you—about them, not you.
- Sing a song to yourself or out loud. Having a favorite song or two on hand is a technique used by lots of athletes to reduce stress and control their level of arousal.

Centering or Re-centering Techniques.

- Visualize a calm, serene place while doing controlled breathing.
- Make a radical change in your physiology. There's a saying, "If it works, don't change anything. If it doesn't work, do anything but what you're doing." Dramatically change whatever it is you're doing with your body. Make some sounds, move some muscles, change your facial

expression, laugh, make physical gestures, change your body position, etc.

- Visualize a perfect skydive. See yourself performing smoothly and effortlessly.

- Pretend you're a skygod. I mean really get into it. Think of yourself as your favorite skydiving hero. Ask yourself the question, "What would he/she be thinking in my situation?" Then think it. Ask yourself, "What would he/she be doing in my situation?" Then do it.

- Repeat affirmations to yourself. "I'm relaxed, I'm calm, I'm focused, I'm confident, I know this skydive inside and out."

- Sometimes the best thing you can do with fear is turn it inside out, accept the challenge it's presenting, and allow yourself to feel the stubbornness of determination. Momentarily clench your fists, raise your voice, tense any and all of the muscles in your body and then release them. Be firm with yourself and refuse to be afraid.

- Change the pictures you're seeing in your mind. Either change the content or the submodalities. (See video game #1, The Director, page 83.)

- Change the questions you're asking yourself. Instead of, "What happens if I fail?" or "Why do I always get nervous and screw up?" ask yourself "How am I going to make this a great skydive?" or "What can I do to make this jump fun?"

All of the above techniques can be used to decrease or eliminate performance anxiety in the plane. The real work, however, begins on the ground and off the drop zone. Each of these methods works, if you work it. Repetition is the key. They should be practiced until they become automatic and available to you on the spot. Just like cutaway procedures, they need to be executed quickly and efficiently. Practice them whenever you get a chance: at home, on the job, in social situations, in traffic, in crowded malls, anywhere.

After experimenting with some of the above techniques you'll find that you like some better than others. Great! Pick a few favorites and learn them thoroughly, until you can use them without hesitation or fumbling. Then you're truly prepared for any emotional emergency. And chances are if you practice them enough, you'll eliminate most, if not all of your performance anxiety to begin with. But if it does show up, your training in emergency procedures will be adequate for the situation.

CHAPTER 11

Attitude and Peak Performance

~The Magic of Reframing~

A young boy approached an old Indian man, having noticed a large and unusual medallion around his neck. As he got closer he could see that engraved in the medallion were two wolves engaged in a fierce battle. Taken by curiosity, the boy asked the Indian why the wolves were fighting. The Indian said, "One is a good wolf who has remarkable vision and clarity of purpose and the other is a bad wolf who is always trying to confuse the good wolf and prevent him from realizing his dreams. They're both very powerful and fight day and night all of the time." With a puzzled look on his face the boy asked, "Does anyone ever win the battle?"
"Oh yes, of course," said the Indian. "Which one?" asked the boy. And the Indian replied, "The one I feed the most."

Unlike a visualization or imagery exercise, real life doesn't allow us to control all the variables in a situation. Instead, life does what it does best—it provides the unexpected.

You're at an important meet and Murphy's Law goes into effect: the weather turns sour, a teammate gets injured, you have an argument with your significant other, the judges are overly harsh in their scoring (or even worse, they're favoring another team), the video camera's got a glitch, your performance is below par and you're furious with yourself, one of your teammates has a hangover, etc. The list is endless.

So how do you stay centered and maintain focus and clarity of purpose when nothing seems to be going the way you planned? How do you not get distracted, frustrated, and annoyed when you're doing your best to remain positive and your best just isn't good enough? While there are no easy answers, there are some simple techniques and ways of thinking that, if practiced on a regular basis, can really make a difference in times like these.

Reframing is a mental tool that involves making a conscious, deliberate choice to change your perception of a situation to one that empowers you rather than one that depletes your energy—to metaphorically put a new, positive frame around the picture you're viewing in your mind's eye. Zig Zeigler, the author and motivational speaker, says, "Positive thinking won't do anything. But it will do everything better than negative thinking." The saying, "I can be unhappy because a rose bush has thorns, or happy because a thorn bush has roses," is a good example of reframing. "Is the glass half empty or half full?" is another. My favorite is, "Life is a series of wonderful opportunities, brilliantly disguised as impossible situations."

Is it really possible, or is it just desperate, wishful thinking to believe that Murphy's Law might be a blessing in disguise, or that "every cloud does have a silver lining"? A commitment to peak performance requires that you ask yourself a few key questions to find the answer. The first is: "How do I benefit by complaining or focusing on unfavorable conditions that I have no control over?" The answer clearly is that there is no benefit. Fixating on something you can't possibly change can only lead to frustration, aggravation, distraction, and an unnecessary expenditure of valuable energy. In other words, it gets you nowhere and even hinders progress. And if you're serious about reaching your goal, then these negative feelings and emotions can't be tolerated. At least for the moment they need to be eliminated or transformed into thoughts, words, and actions that enhance your performance and drive you forward. Under difficult conditions though, this can only be achieved by asking yourself the second and most important question: "How can I find opportunity in this situation?"

There are experts at creating opportunity and there are amateurs. Find a winner—a champion—and you'll find an expert. They achieve what others consider impossible because they subscribe to a powerful belief that allows them to transcend any situation and emerge with greater strength and abilities. They have an unwavering conviction that *opportunity can be created out of any situation—with no exceptions—no matter how bad it may seem.*

Winners judge nothing as hopeless and refuse to see themselves as victims, regardless of the circumstances. They have no time for regret or remorse, they consider failure simply as another form of feedback for learning, and they welcome unusual and unexpected results.

On the other hand, there are people whose belief systems cause them to be easily defeated by life—those who constantly feel victimized by circumstances. They choose to interpret life in a way that cripples their ability to advance in difficult times. These individuals don't realize that it's their choice of perception—the meaning they give to a situation— that creates their misery even more than the situation itself, and that it's their own resignation and sense of hopelessness that blocks them from reaching their goal or achieving their full potential.

Those of us who have experienced this debilitating state of mind know how easily it can engulf us and how difficult it can be to escape. Few of us are born with a natural immunity to this condition though some of us may have had the benefit of powerful and positive role models over the years. It takes a lot of hard mental work and perseverance to avoid falling into this trap. The antidote is accepting responsibility for how we interpret life. Only then can we see that by changing our perception we greatly improve our ability to respond to life and to reach our goals.

How and why this works.
Every experience has positive and negative aspects. Both are real; both are valid. The side you choose to pay attention to is the side that will grow and have an affect on you. What you focus on, enlarges. So when life gives you lemons, lemonade is a possibility—but only if you choose it.

If you don't choose positively, you wind up walking around with a bitter taste in your mouth looking for someone or something to blame for your misfortune. The result is an enormous waste of time and energy. The author Lewis F. Presnall, inflicted with polio as a child, decided early in his illness that whenever he thought of something he couldn't do, he would immediately think of something he could do. This reframing came out of his commitment to design the outcome of his own life and not be victimized by circumstances.

Bruce Jenner, the decathlon gold medal winner at the 1976 Montreal Olympics had this to say:

> I determine my future. I don't let anything on the outside of me determine my future. I'm in control. The crowd doesn't have anything to do with it, the other competitors don't have anything to do with it, the jet that's flying overhead doesn't have anything to do with it. If I'm going to do well, it's going to come from inside of me. That's what's going to determine it. So you just focus. Everything just goes "zip," right inside. (Jones, 58)

Consider the 1999 U.S. Nationals in Florida. For the most part it was a week of clouds and rain—a waiting game that left many competitors angry, annoyed, and disgusted, not to mention distracted and out of focus when they finally did get in the air.

Noticing my own attitude begin to deteriorate after a few days, I decided that whenever I caught myself in negative thinking, I would immediately ask, "What can this experience teach me? What can I learn from being here that I wouldn't be able to learn if this weren't happening?" I began making a list of the possible benefits I could derive from being at this wet, soggy event. I could:

- Learn patience and increase my tolerance for discomfort.
- Improve my ability to remain focused and centered under adverse conditions.
- Use my time on the ground to meet new people and deepen existing relationships, which I might not have a chance to do otherwise.
- Observe competitors who were successful at staying centered and relaxed and ask them how they do it.
- Find people who were having a hard time and possibly help them out by sharing what works for me.

At every moment there was a choice to focus on what I could do or what I couldn't do. Since I knew I couldn't change the picture, I decided to change the frame. The best example of reframing I heard that week came during a conversation I had with a top competitor. When the subject of lousy whether came up, this jumper smiled and said cheerfully, "I love this kind of weather. I've always loved competing under these conditions because it throws everybody off. People get distracted and their performance shows it. I just sit back and enjoy the advantage it gives me."

Now that's a powerful reframe.

The Beginning

God,
if life is so many things that I am not, and never will be,
give me the strength to be what I am.
Gabriela Brimmer

For some this is an end; for others it's just a beginning. Peak performance is not a destination but a journey—a way of life. We can use all the tools, techniques, methods, systems, and procedures available to accomplish a goal; we can buy the latest and most advanced equipment and be trained and coached by the best in the world. But unless we are living a life of peak performance, a life committed to being the best we can be in everything we do, then our achievements will never be what they could be, no matter how glorious.

For some this is a book about skydiving; for others it's a book about life. Some people believe that they can be outstanding in one area of life while careless and thoughtless in another, and they certainly can, but not without paying a price. The cost is damage to the integrity and focus of their highest purpose.

It saddens me to see so much wasted talent, energy, intelligence, and creativity. It saddens me to realize how much of my life I've squandered avoiding situations I knew I needed to confront, or refusing help out of fear of embarrassment, or not asking questions because I worried they might sound stupid, or all the times I put my image (who I thought I should be) ahead of my passion and spirit because I needed to look good.

Now, when I think of those times, I wish I had learned some lessons earlier in my life. I wish I had developed more discipline, practiced greater courage, followed my passion at all cost, and discovered a deeper appreciation for integrity in thought, word and action. I wish.

But if I learn these lessons now then nothing is wasted, because now is all there is. Now is the only reality that exists. Now is all I have.

And so I invite you to join me in cultivating a peak performance life in everything you do. Not a life that is stiflingly serious or about constantly striving for perfection, but a life based on joy and the fulfillment of dreams—a life committed to "accepting the challenge," whatever that challenge may be today.

Together we can confront that challenge passionately, one moment at a time, with a *knowing* that victory is ours, even if the outcome is other than what we desired or expected. And while losing is never enjoyable or welcomed, the greatest thing any man or woman can ever profess at the end of a contest is, "I did my best."

Resolve says, "I will."

The man says, "I will climb this mountain. They told me it is too high, too far, too steep, too rocky and too difficult. But it's my mountain. I will climb it. You will soon see me waving from the top or dead on the side from trying."
(Jim Rohn)

References and Suggested Reading

Bassham, Lanny. *With Winning in Mind.* San Antonio: XPress, 1988.

Clarkson, Michael. *Competitive Fire.* Champaign, IL: Human Kinetics, 1999.

Csikszentmihalyi, Mihaly. *Flow: The Psychology of Optimal Experience.* New York: Harper and Row, 1990.

Cooper, Andrew. *Playing in the Zone.* Boston: Shambhala, 1998.

Daggett, Tim and Jean Stone. *Dare to Dream.* New York: Wynwood, 1992.

Jackson, Phil. *Sacred Hoops.* New York: Hyperion, 1995.

Jackson, Susan and Mihaly Csikszentmihalyi. *Flow in Sports.* Champaign, IL: Human Kinetics, 1999.

Jones, Charlie. *What Makes Winners Win.* New York: Broadway Books, 1997.

Loehr, James. *The New Toughness Training for Sports.* New York: Plume, 1994.

Orlick, Terry. *In Pursuit of Excellence.* Champaign, IL: Leisure Press, 1990.

Riley, Pat. *The Winner Within.* New York: Berkley, 1993.

Russell, Bill and Taylor Branch. *Second Wind.* New York: Random House, 1979.

Williams, Pat. *The Magic of Teamwork.* Nashville: Thomas Nelson Inc., 1997.

Ungerleider, Steven. *Mental Training for Peak Performance.* Emmaus, PA: Rodale Press, 1996.

Capacchione, Lucia. *Visioning.* New York: Jeremy P. Tarcher/Putnam, 2000.

ABOUT THE AUTHOR

John DeRosalia MSW, C.Ht., affectionately referred to as "Dr. John" in the skydiving community (even though he is not a doctor) is a Peak Performance Specialist and Consultant as well as a psychotherapist, hypnotherapist, author, motivational speaker, and skydiver. In professional practice for over twenty-six years and founder of SkyMind School of Peak Performance, John has been the mental training coach for numerous world-class teams and individuals, among them World Cup Champions Generation FX, the British National Team (Sebastian XL), the U.S. Army Parachute Team (The Golden Knights), and the U.S. Parachute Team. He maintains a private practice in upstate New York and travels worldwide to coach and present his curriculum to a wide variety of athletes, business professionals and various other groups.

John DeRosalia * PO Box 283 * West Hurley, NY 12491
USA
Phone and Fax: (845) 331-8384
Email: skymind@pobox.com